Praise for
MY FATHER'S HAND

"My Father's Hand is a love story written from the heart of one who knows the Author of love. Inspiring, encouraging and informative, Naomi Rhode enriches us as she reveals the impact her earthly father had on her and then helps open the door to Heaven, lighting the path to peace on earth and eternal joy."

Zig Ziglar, Author/Motivational Teacher

"Naomi Rhode's new book MY FATHER'S HAND is entirely engaging. From her brother she received the gift of her father's sermons delivered over a period of time sixty years ago. Reliving these messages after so many years stimulated memory of her childhood now seen through the passage of time. She shares her father's words and responds with her own reflections which are poignant and reflective. MY FATHER'S HAND is a tribute to a father and a declaration of Naomi's faith. I was very moved by the two voices, and I carry with me a deep sense of the family's roots and treasure. A wonderful read."

Elizabeth Peale Allen, Chairman of the Board of Guideposts

One of the most beautiful love stories I've ever read. It is a symphony of God's love revealed through the relationship of a father and daughter. Even though the father is taken from her at a young age, his love and wisdom lives on in her. This book will bless and inspire every reader to think more seriously of the importance of building relatio   eternal values.

Charles "T" Jones, CPAE, RFC
Author of *Life is Tremendous*

"This book is a treasure for all time! Naomi's inspiring words will touch your heart, nourish your mind, and nurture your soul. Read these pages to learn . . . read them again to grow."

Nido R. Qubein
President, High Point University
Chairman, Great Harvest Bread Co.

"You are about to meet Virgil Reed, an amazing man of God, whose heartfelt messages are filled with genuine compassion and deep conviction. And you will meet his daughter, Naomi Rhode, an equally gifted wordsmith, who brings fresh insights from her earthly father's words and her heavenly Father's Word as well. Together, father and daughter sing in harmony across the decades, demonstrating the timelessness of God's truth and the impact one man's faith can have on generations to come. A truly unique and inspiring work!"

Liz Curtis Higgs
Author of *Unveiling Mary Magdalene*

My Father's Hand

A Daughter's Reflections
On A Father's Wisdom

My Father's Hand
A Daughter's Reflections On A Father's Wisdom

By
Naomi Rhode, CSP,
CPAE Speaker Hall of Fame

**Executive
Books**

MY FATHER'S HAND

Published by
Executive Books
206 West Allen Street
Mechanicsburg, PA 17055

Copyright © 2006 by Naomi Rhode

ISBN: 1-933715-08-1

Cover Design and Interior Layout by Gregory Dixon

Cover Photo: Virgil and Naomi (Father and Daughter)

Printed in the United States of America

Dedication

My Father's Hand

Gratitude to God
for His inheritance
which He blessed me with
through the lives of Virgil and Ellen Reed

This 'precious gift' Jim and I pass on to our children:
Mark, Beth, and Katherine.

And to our grandchildren: Titus and Meridien Rhode;
Dathan, Carsten, Quinlan, Kylin, Stenson and
Wynston Hamann; Karl, Haaken, Hannah and Broder
Magnuson.

Omer and Marcia Reed have passed this 'gift' on to
their children: Karl, Kelly, Kevin, Kirsten & Kary.
And to their grandchildren: Kyle, Kasey, Katy,
Kristoffer, Kory, and Kirsten Reed.

*"Oh Lord, You are the portion of my inheritance and
my cup—Yes I have a good inheritance."*

Psalm 16:5a, 16:6b

Acknowledgements
For
'My Father's Hand'

We celebrate biological family!
We celebrate the Family of God!
And, we celebrate those who 'come alongside,' encouraging, helping, bringing expertise, organizational skills, and the 'inspiration' we
need to begin and complete a project.

My number one encourager has been my husband, Jim, who has
believed in this project, encouraged and empowered its completion.

My thanks to my Chaber Sisters, Mary Malouf, Naomi Van Liew,
Donna Otto, Sandy Lane, and Joan Malouf who always believe in the
World Vision of Ministry 'outside the organized church' that I feel
called to.

My thanks to my Summit Sisters, Liz Curtis Higgs, Glenna Salsbury,
Gail Wenos, and Elizabeth Jeffries Tweed, who as speakers and
authors have brainstormed lovingly the concept and impact of this
book.

Special thanks to my Master Mind Group of Professional Speakers,
'Speakers Roundtable' for their visioning and sound professional
guidance.

Prayerful gratitude to our Bible Study Group of more than 15 years,
Newmans, Masons, Cooks, Watkins, Parlettes, Hermansons, Paula
Smith, Pulsifers and Hildebrands for their spiritual guidance and
prayers.

My thanks to my brother, Omer Reed, who saved my Dad's sermons
carefully in their 'yellowed' numbered envelopes, and presented
them to me after a speaking engagement at his seminar—a huge
surprise and a very emotional 'gift.'

My thanks to Virginia Kail who did the original transcribing of the sermons.

My thanks to my Professional Writer/Speaker Colleague, Bob Kelly, who spent endless hours reading, organizing and entering all my Dad's sermons in the computer. His editing skills are wondrous! His wisdom is priceless. And the fact that he truly "fell in love with my Dad" and looks forward to meeting him in Heaven someday is an awesome encouragement to me.

Mostly, I acknowledge the rich heritage, modeling, mentoring and 'platform privilege' that my Father, Virgil Asbury Reed, and my Mother, Mabel Ellenborg Goodman Reed, gave to me. Their mutual influence is indelibly imprinted on my soul.

Thank you, God, for each of these empowering people in my life.

Surely, as it says in the Psalms, "The boundary lines of my life have been drawn in very pleasant places."

Naomi Rhode, CSP, CPAE Speaker Hall of Fame

Table of Contents

Prologue

Words of Wisdom from Virgil Reed

- We must change ourselves to fit the suit that has been made for us by the Master Fitter.

- There were plenty of other healers and teachers, but only one Jesus. He was and is a combination of power and tireless love.

- When God would accomplish a great task, He does not resort to the spectacular, nor does He send legions of soldiers. He puts His plan in a mother's mind, lays a baby in her arms, and waits.

- Words are only air converted into sound, but their meaning and the intent of the heart that caused them to be uttered is impossible to erase, as it is to recapture an extinguished flame.

- Yesterday is a memory; tomorrow is an imagination; today is eternity. Cut out two days of your life, yesterday with its mistakes, tomorrow with its fears, and live only today.

- There is one name [Jesus] that is altogether lovely, too lovely to be handled lightly.

- We must take that name with us along with our own name.

- Men are tempted, not on the side of their weakness, but on the side of their power. The orator is tempted to be too eloquent, the soldier to fight too often.

- If we listen to the same pilot who spoke peace to an unquiet sea for the disciples, if we listen to the Master who advised Paul, then our sailing will be secure and the landing will be safe on the other shore.

- How much money do you have in your pocket: $100? $10? $1? 1 Cent? You're that much richer than the millionaire who died last night.

- Christ should and must be as near to you and to me as though He were here in this room with us, or as though He lived in our home.

- It was expedient that He [Jesus] should go away, but will He find you and me still watching when He comes for us?

- Let us challenge every habit, every thought, every emotion, every fear, every worry with, "Halt! Who goes there?" Allow none to enter except to contribute to our well-being.

- Every home should have its family altar where the family may gather at least once each day. In these busy days, many family altars have been replaced, as were those in Israel's days, by altars to gold and lust and worldly amusement.

- The tragedy of many lives is not that our talents are few, but that too frequently we do not use the ones entrusted to us. We pray for bigger opportunities but do not make use of the opportunities that lie in our paths.

- God's use of little things reveals unmistakably His plan and purpose. We say, "It happened." God says, "It came to pass."

- When you cease to praise God from whom all blessings flow for His wonderful loving-kindness…when there is no gratitude for the innumerable blessings of God, you are drifting dangerously near the pit.

- At the cost of many lives, salvation was brought to you. What are you doing with it? What will you do with Jesus?

Neutral you cannot be. Perhaps it's not what will I do with Jesus, but what will He do with me?

- The oil of God's grace and power in the lamp of our lives will light our way through the open doors of happy, useful living as we walk in the steps of the Master.

- Christ is the same today as He was yesterday. He is as ready to bless and save now as He was 20 centuries ago. He still honors faith wherever He finds it.

- How strange it is that an intelligent man, skilled in workmanship, provident in plans, and farseeing in building, is the only creature that is afraid God will not provide, and is unwilling to trust God.

Preface

We look back over 60 years to events brought to our attention by typewritten 3x5 cards, calendared in a small box labeled "1941-1945." Along with the aging card-file, we only see through the window of reality provided by our adult mind, seeking the meaning experienced by our child.

Fortunately there is a golden thread that weaves itself through the fabric of words and time, a remnant if you choose to see it, from the same source that generated the story about to be experienced.

The 60-plus years are but a tick of God's second hand; the message of His word, then and now, remains as it was two thousand years ago. This book may not make the New York Times' best seller list, or be in one's lap with a bowl of popcorn seated in front of a glowing fireplace. Its fire, however, will never go out. It will serve the generations to which it is now being gifted. Those having experienced Virgil Reed are "refugees" on this planet, a planet which now belongs to the generations to whom this book will undoubtedly be a useful and appreciated treasure.

Omer K. Reed, D.D.S.

Introduction

Virgil Asbury Reed was my father, my DAD! And—I was born on his birthday! He seemed really proud of that fact, and we celebrated our birthdays together each year, with great ceremony. May 23rd was truly OUR DAY!

What a thrill to always be "Daddy's girl." He called me his "Little Flicka," and surrounded me with arms, lap and heart of love.

My dad was a giant of a man! His life philosophies, his character, his genuine zest for life, his charisma, his speaking excellence, his love for family, his wisdom, his storytelling ("to cement life's teachable moments," he'd say), and his faith in God were the foundational elements of my childhood.

Having lived through the "Great Depression" in our country (about which he was always willing to share stories), he had a true appreciation of thrift. But far beyond thrift was a philosophy of giving. He'd often tell the story of the shopkeeper during the Great Depression (and I can still hear him 'roll' the "Gr" in Great as he told the story):

> "This shopkeeper was different than all the other shopkeepers in town. *(That seemed to be the key for much of my father's philosophy, going opposite to the grain, choosing to be special/unique.)*
>
> "When you came into his shop to buy five pounds of coffee beans, he would take his marvelous scale and put a five-pound weight on one side, and the empty container on the other. Then, he would ceremoniously put the scoop into the bag of freshly roasted coffee beans, scooping and scooping until the once empty container was perfectly balanced with the five-pound weight.
>
> "The shopkeeper would then pause—and 'twinkle' *(my father seemed to delight in the 'twinkle' part of the story, emphasizing that life with charisma/fun/lightheartedness is indeed part of the 'gift')*, and dip the scoop into the bag of beans one more time. With a smile, he would empty that extra scoop of coffee beans on top of what he had so carefully measured, overflowing the container and tipping the scales in favor of you, the customer.

"As he smiled and 'twinkled,' he would say *'Lagniappe,'* which in French Creole means: 'every bit you paid for, and then just a little bit extra.' It was obviously that 'little bit extra' which had created, built and successfully retained the business other shops lost during that difficult time in our nation's history."

In telling that story, my dad was extremely convincing! He assured me I would be happy, successful, and even significant in life's journey if I regularly gave 'every bit I was paid for, and then a little bit extra'—in my personal life, in my business life, with friends, and with family.

Dad died when I was only thirteen, but, every day, I can still hear his echo in my soul: "The only thing you can really keep in life is what you give away!"

During his all too brief life, my dad gave me everything he had—or so I thought. Then, in 2001, nearly a half-century after his death, my brother, Omer K. Reed, presented me with a priceless gift, the notes from more than 150 of my dad's messages—to the congregations he served, to the Boy Scouts he trained, and to the "Come and See" adult Bible studies he taught.

As I read them today, and share them with you, so many years after he died, I can almost see him looking down at us from Heaven and saying, with a twinkle in his eye, *"Lagniappe!"*

What a wonderful model for all of us to follow in our lives: May each of us be a *Lagniappe* person, "giving every bit we've paid for, and just a little bit extra!"

Chapter

1

The Risen Christ

"Joseph of Arimathea, a prominent member of the Council, who was himself waiting for the kingdom of God, went boldly to Pilate and asked for Jesus' body. Pilate was surprised to hear that he was already dead. Summoning the centurion, he asked him if Jesus had already died. When he learned from the centurion that it was so, he gave the body to Joseph. So Joseph brought some linen cloth, took down the body, wrapped it in the linen, and placed it in a tomb cut out of the rock. Then he rolled a stone against the entrance of the tomb."

Mark 15:43-46

For you and for me, is Jesus risen? With the rising of each morning's sun, we're reminded of that resurrection.

(Virgil Reed)

Into my twelve-year-old heart, stressed with the trauma of loss and uncertainty, came an overwhelming, knowing peace. The verifying resurrection of my faith—daddies who love Jesus don't die!

(Naomi Reed Rhode)

Our Lord has written the promise of the resurrection, not in books alone, but in every leaf in springtime.

Martin Luther

Before there can be a resurrection, there is always a death. In the fall comes the low, systematic dying in the realm of nature. The wheat, the corn, the fruit of the orchard and garden yield to death. It's God's plan and way.

Jesus Christ submitted to the Divine will and plan, and suffered death on the cross for the sins of the world, but also that over death there might be a victory—that there might be a resurrection.

On that first Easter morning, after the Sabbath had passed, Mary Magdalene, Mary the mother of James, and Salome had come through chill and the dew and had brought with them spices to anoint Jesus' body.

But had Jesus not said that death could not hold Him? Could they not believe His statement? They did, and they didn't. They had seen death before, and had tenderly cared for corpse after corpse of loved ones and friends.

And now Jesus was dead. They would not spare their embalming spices for this, the greatest of all bodies.

At the first break of day, at the rising of the sun, can you see them? Little sleep and many tears, and now they are saying something: "Who will roll the stone away from the entrance of the tomb?"

Daily we find ourselves in like circumstances, the seemingly impossible standing in our way, and then something happens. It happened that morning for those three women for, when they looked, they saw that the stone was rolled away.

Entering the tomb, they saw a young man clothed in white, who said to them: "You seek Jesus of Nazareth (Can that be said of us?) who was crucified. He is risen!"

For you and for me, is Jesus risen? With the rising of each morning's sun, we're reminded of that resurrection. The bursting forth of grass and flowers and buds and leaves all tell us in their silent way that each day can be an Easter day if, for us, Christ has been raised from the dead.

After the gladness of that first Easter morning experience, the three women were instructed to go and tell His disciples—and Peter.

How sad are those last two words. Was Peter no longer a disciple, for he had denied his Lord and Master?

Is there a Peter here this morning? If there is, there is for you these gracious words: "Repent and believe and you shall be saved."

As Christ was raised from the dead, may we also rise in newness of life. May we rise from this Easter day to newness of service. And because of His death on the cross and His victory over death, may we so live in nearness to Him that we too may rise in newness of life when these mortal bodies shall serve us no more.

(Excerpted from a message by Virgil Reed, given on April 1, 1945.)

Naomi Responds

Easter morning is not merely a declaration that we are immortal, but a declaration that we are the immortal children of God.

George Matheson

Why do we call it 'Good Friday?' I wondered. Is it because school is out? Or because we can shop for our Easter finery, color eggs, or prepare for a family celebration? Certainly it isn't because we believe it's 'good' that Christ was mocked, battered and crucified, is it?

That 'Good Friday' was a beautiful spring day. I was thirteen, mature for my age, and in love with life, family, friends, school, and music. A strong cocoon and strong cords of loving security were mine. Though my mother had been very ill with a heart condition, my strong, charismatic, storytelling daddy was the fixer, provider, rewarder, and teacher/mentor in my life. Educator, ordained minister and professional Boy Scout executive were his titles. Tenderness, wisdom, humor, character and Godliness were his armor. To me, he was bigger than life! Indestructible!

The day before that 'Good Friday,' our family was happy. I practiced the piano for two hours. I wanted my rendition of "The Holy City," for the offertory at the Easter worship service to echo the pathos, the drama, and the feeling of my faith. It was a musical portrayal of Christ's last week on earth—the most important week in history. Could a 13-year-old girl portray such emotion?

Mother baked brown bread in round cans with raisins and nuts—an Easter tradition. My brother and dad drove to the desert to purchase and transplant orange trees in our yard.

Supper (as transplanted Midwesterners call it) was a casserole and Jell-O salad. It was relaxed and happy until....

"I have a terrible headache, Ellen. I must lie down on the davenport," Daddy said.

Within minutes, the right side of his body was paralyzed and his consciousness gone! I remember riding barefoot to the hospital. Shoes didn't seem important. Nothing did for now.

The night was long.

The next morning, that 'Good Friday,' a neighbor took me to a scheduled dental appointment. Mother was there to pick me up afterward, and to tell me, "Your Daddy just died of a massive stroke."

I went home to my bedroom, wondering about grieving, death, reality, life. It didn't seem real. Suddenly, I knew why—because he wasn't really dead! I knew what no one else seemed to know. My Daddy would rise from the dead on Easter Sunday, just as Christ had.

I didn't need to grieve. I could play the piano without faltering, in my brand-new white eyelet dress. Why didn't others seem to share this hope? This belief? Maybe I shouldn't tell them what I know will happen—that daddies like mine don't really die!

So, I didn't tell them. I kept all those things and "pondered them in my heart." It was my secret, my joy! Others seemed critical of my lack of grieving as Friday afternoon, evening, and Saturday passed. I knew that on that first Easter morning, when the women went to mourn, they were met by angels. The stone sealing the grave had been rolled away. Jesus wasn't there—He was risen!

Early that Easter morning I awoke, expectant, not mourning, to see "the stone rolled away," to see my Daddy—to know again his love and care for his "Little Flicka."

But he wasn't there. He wasn't risen!

Or – wait – was he?

Did Christ not say, "You shall not die, you shall be changed. Those of you who believe in what I say and what I did for you on the cross that 'Good Friday' will also be raised with me to life everlasting." Christ arose! We sing, "Hallelujah!"

And into my thirteen-year-old heart, stressed with the trauma of loss and uncertainty, came an overwhelming, knowing peace. The verifying resurrection of my faith—daddies who love Jesus don't die! They go to turn on the lights in the mansions of glory.

That day was, indeed, a 'Good Friday!'

Chapter
2
In the Beginning
Was the Word

"The Word became flesh and lived for a while among us…"

John 1:14

Jesus showed great range of emotions in His words. When He whispered, Simon wept and John sobbed. When He thundered, Lazarus came forth from the tomb.

(Virgil Reed)

As I picture the reality of the echo within me of my earthly father's words, and my Heavenly Father's words, I again focus on the privilege and the power of words.

(Naomi Reed Rhode)

**Let us encourage ourselves in the Lord. How much
He encouraged others! On the stormy lake, and in
the upper room. He spoke words of cheer to the
paralytic, and to the stricken woman. He
administered words of comfort.**

Arthur Soutter

D id you ever think of Jesus as an orator? From Scripture, we
can see that he was a popular speaker—convincing, dynamic and positive:

- "So many gathered that there was no room left, not even
  outside the door, and he preached the word to them." (Mark
  2:2)
- "...crowds of people came to hear him..." (Luke 5:15)
- "All spoke well of him and were amazed at the gracious
  words that came from his lips..." (Luke 4:22)
- "They were amazed at his teaching, because his message
  had authority." (Luke 4:32)

Jesus had great appeal among the common people, who heard him
gladly. In Chapter 12 of his gospel, Luke reports that "a crowd of
many thousands, so that they were trampling on one another" had
gathered to hear him speak (vs.1). Even his enemies testified to his
ability. When the chief priests and the Pharisees sent temple guards
to arrest him, their excuse for returning empty-handed was, "No one
ever spoke the way this man does."

Jesus' words were not only unusual but sensational, arousing
emotions ranging from enthusiastic commendation to bitter hostility.
Whether in one-on-one situations, or seated around a supper table, or
in public forums, Jesus seized every opportunity to share his message, focusing always on spiritual matters. Whether speaking to
Nicodemus, the rich young ruler, the Samaritan woman at the well,
his disciples or huge crowds, he spoke to them personally: you, you,
you—never I, I, I.

Jesus spoke directly, forcefully, and with both conviction and
compassion. He was not afraid to criticize the religious leaders of the
day in the strongest possible language, denouncing their hypocrisy,
while knowing full well the price he would have to pay for his out-

spokenness. At the same time, he spoke as one who loved God and men, showing great compassion for the sick and the suffering.

Jesus showed great range of emotion in his words. When He whispered, Simon wept and John sobbed. When he thundered, Lazarus came forth from the tomb.

This Jesus is still a preacher and an orator, speaking quietly to your heart and soul. What has he said, and what is he saying to you and me today? Listen to his words:

- "I am the light of the world." (John 12:12)
- "I have come that they may have life, and have it to the full." (John 10:10)
- "Do to others what you would have them do to you." (Matt. 7:12)
- "Come to me." (Matt. 11:28)
- "He who is not with me is against me." (Matt. 12:30)
- "Whatever you did for one of the least of these brothers of mine, you did for me." (Matt. 25:40)
- "Ask and it will be given to you." (Matt. 7:7)
- "Love your enemies." (Luke 6:27)
- "But I, if I be lifted up from the earth, will draw all men to myself." (John 12:32)
- "I am the resurrection and the life." ((John 11:25)
- "What good is it for a man to gain the whole world, yet forfeit his soul?" (Mark 8:36)

These are Christ's messages. Let us hear and obey, and rejoice and love and live.

(Excerpted from a message by Virgil Reed, given on January 21, 1945.)

Naomi Responds

All our words will be useless unless they come from within—words which do not give the light of Christ increase the darkness.

Mother Teresa

Certainly it's hard to recognize that the "voice" you once heard is still resounding with a clarified message of purpose. However, when I again read my Dad's message about words, and how Jesus speaks to you and me, I'm not surprised.

I'm not surprised that without planning to, I became a professional speaker. Not surprised that the passion within me has led me to speak somewhere, almost every week, for more than 30 years. Not surprised that I'd become active in the National Speakers Association, 4,000 people who share this passion for words, and become their national president. And, not surprised, reflectively, that I chose for my theme as president, "The Privilege of the Platform."

My inspiration was a great speaker, orator, yes—my father. But, much, much more, he introduced me to "The Master Speaker," the One who "spoke" and the world came into being. The One who "spoke," and the sea parted for His people to pass through. The One who "spoke," and Lazarus was raised from the dead. The One who "spoke," and the thief was promised eternity with His Father in heaven. AND, the One who spoke quietly to my heart and gave me life eternal.

And, the message I hear is that we're to "go and do likewise," extending hope, light, love, care, purpose, and grace on all the platforms of our world, with incredible "privilege."

As I picture the reality of the echo within me of my earthly father's words, and my Heavenly Father's words, I again focus on the privilege and the power of words.

As children, we sing the little song, "Sticks and stones may break my bones, but words will never hurt me." As adults we know that song isn't true.

We know words hurt as well as heal. We know words kill as well as caress. We know words are the gift wrapping around relationships which inspire and instruct.

What are the echoes I'm originating in the souls of my listeners?

What are the words I give as gifts? Do I really know that "words become frozen reality," and that "The Privilege of the Platform" for each of us in our personal/professional worlds is a high honor, to be prized as precious gold! It makes no difference if we're speaking to hundreds sitting in an auditorium, or to a neighbor sitting across the table, or to our children. No matter who, or how many, are in our audience, may our speech be filled with words of encouragement, compassion, praise and love.

Chapter
3
The Danger
Of Delay

"Now there were four men with leprosy at the entrance of the city gate. They said to each other, 'Why stay here until we die? If we say, we'll go into the city— the famine is there, and we will die. And if we stay here, we will die. So let's go over to the camp of the Arameans and surrender. If they spare us, we live; if they kill us, then we die."

2 Kings 7:3-4

"And now what are you waiting for? Get up, be baptized and wash your sins away, calling on his name."

Acts 22:16

There is danger and death, eternal death in delay.
Procrastination is deadly. Why linger longer?

(Virgil Reed)

Some wait, procrastinate, delay, one second too
long, and miss the "Come unto Me," that grace-
filled invitation of life here, and life hereafter.

(Naomi Reed Rhode)

**God has promised forgiveness to your repentance, but
He has not promised tomorrow to your procrastination.**

Saint Augustine

O ne of the most subtle temptations Satan presents to the lost is
that of waiting. Procrastination is not only the thief of time
but of souls. It is far worse than that. In the words of another, "I wish it were no worse than a thief. It is a murderer; and that
which it kills is not time merely but immortal souls."

Four Lepers! When the city of Samaria closed its gates, four lepers who had sat at one of the gates begging found their source of revenue cut off. From day to day, they sat there, growing hungry—leaner, lankier, and more needy every day that passed. Finally, one said, "Why stay here until we die? If we sit here we die." That was most certain.

There were three courses open to them. They could stay where they were—and die. They could go into the city, but the famine was on. Or they could venture out on faith and throw themselves on the mercy of the Syrian army.

We do Scripture no injury when we let these four lepers stand for lost men and women and put in their hearts this question: "Why stay here until we die?" The soul with one sin unforgiven is surely dying.

It takes only one sin unforgiven to damn a soul. One hole in the Titanic was enough to sink it. One bullet through the heart is enough to kill. One grain of poison is enough to bring death. God says, "If one should keep the whole law and yet offend in one point, he is become guilty of all."

"Why stay here until we die? What are you waiting for? Arise and be baptized."

Something many lost souls say is, "I'm not fit." It's not a matter of being fit but being willing to be made fit. Christ came into this world to seek and save the unfit. If He hadn't come to save the unfit, He would never have saved me.

Paul's hands were red with his fellow man's blood. He felt he was the very chief of sinners. If ever a man was unfit, he was. God doesn't say, "Whosoever is fit, but whosoever will, let him take the water of life freely."

It's not unfitness but the unwillingness to be made fit that's the trouble. Our very unfitness is a recommendation to God's mercy.

It's told that a boy, ragged, dirty, with bare head, bare feet, and deserted look, came to an orphanage. He knocked on the door and the superintendent answered. He asked the boy what he wanted. The boy replied that he wanted to be admitted.

The superintendent asked, "What recommendations have you?" He replied that if his bare head, dirty face, ragged clothes, and bare feet didn't recommend him, he had none. The door was thrown wide open, and the superintendent said, "Come in, my boy, come in."

"Why stay here until you die? What are you waiting for? Why do you tarry so long?" Don't let it be said of you, "While I was busy here and there, He was gone."

There is danger and death, eternal death in delay. Procrastination is often fatal. Postponement is deadly. Why linger longer? Why loiter till later? Why defer a single moment? Those who come to the end of the way unsaved must say, "The harvest is passed, the summer is ended, and I am not saved."

"Why stay here until we die?" "Why wait any longer?" "What am I waiting for, my hope is in thee?" "Come, for all things are now ready." "And whosoever will, let him take the water of life freely."

(Excerpted from a message by Virgil Reed, given on July 15, 1945.)

Naomi Responds

By the streets of "by and by," one arrives
at the house of "never."

Spanish Proverb

In my journal, I have a back page for the people in my life whom I cherish, who've left this earth for eternity. I haven't always done that—just the last couple years. I'm not sure why I'm doing it. Maybe because I finally figured out that it's part of life—part of living to pass from this existence to the next—part of the journey from one shore to the next. One breath on earth, the next in eternity. That as each of us is born, each of us will die. That as Scripture tells us, "There is a time for everything…a time to be born, and a time to die" (Ecclesiastes 3:1-2)

Maybe it's because in some indelible way, I want to remember their names, the dates of their birth and death, their age of departure from this earth, and their deep significance in my life. What I'm learning is that they're all ages when they leave earth, and that for most, it's unplanned, unexpected, and beyond their control.

What I'm also learning is that they've all had a lifelong call on their lives "to come, just as they are." To respond to the Father's invitation.

I'm also learning that they *all* want to live eternally with their Creator—but some wait, procrastinate, delay, one second too long, and miss the "Come unto Me," that grace-filled invitation of life here, and life hereafter.

When we delay, I have to believe it's out of ignorance of the abundance of life NOW in the "coming." As much as we abhor much of the procrastination and the "thief of time" in our daily lives, we must consider the monumental price—eternally—of the procrastination that leads to the "thief of a soul."

You've been there—I've been there—the bedside, the last days, hours, and moments on earth of a friend or family member who had responded to the Father's invitation. We've seen the total peace and joy in the eyes of those who had answered "Yes" to the "Come, come to Me, and I will give you peace."

The morning my mother, Ellen Reed, died, after a long illness, she announced, "I am going to die today." She went on to say I'd been a wonderful daughter. She gave me some last-minute instructions, much as you would if you were leaving your child for a business trip. She then looked up to the ceiling (and beyond, no doubt), and said, "the Lord be praised, the Lord be praised," and she died.

There was peace as His arms reached out to lift her soul to a final gentle "Come, come home, Ellen. I have prepared a place for you," from her loving eternal Father.

And though I was obviously stunned and grief-stricken, I sat in overwhelming amazement. I'd seen with my own eyes the reward of living in His love, and dying in His arms and in His grace.

Will I see her again? Will you see your loved ones again?

My mother and father both made sure I hadn't "procrastinated." They knew the danger of delay. They made sure I had come to my heavenly Father, in all my unworthiness, been accepted by His love, and that indeed we would share eternity with one another, and with the Father. Is there greater peace than that on this earth?

Thanks, Dad, for the sermon on delay, on procrastination! You, no doubt, are cheering us on, from the grandstands above, grateful to God for His call on our lives, and our response in a humble, unworthy "Yes," with no delay, much as the thief on the cross to whom Jesus said, "This day you will be with me in Paradise."

Chapter
4
The Man
Who Lost
His Dream

"For Demas, because he loved this world, has deserted me…"

2 Timothy 4:10

God sent you a great moment. He gave you a dream of what you might be and do—don't lose it!

(Virgil Reed)

"To Dream the Impossible Dream" echoes in our hearts when we hear the call of God, and we view a hurting world!

(Naomi Reed Rhode)

> **Hold fast to dreams**
> **For if dreams die**
> **Life is a broken-winged bird**
> **That cannot fly.**
>
> *Langston Hughes*

Less than a dozen words, yet what a long story they could tell if we had the key to them. Paul didn't write just to fill up the space allotted. Paul wrote that entry in pain. Dare we read between the lines? Yes.

Demas was the man who lost his dream, not a sleeping dream, but a waking dream, a dream in the light of day, a hope, a longing. He had to have had a dream, or else Paul could not have written, "Demas has deserted me."

A "daydream" is a reverent term, a period in which the soul rises to breathe. The dreams recorded in Scripture were perhaps more daydreams than night dreams. You can't read the Bible and leave out the dreams: Jacob's ladder at Bethel; Joseph's strange glimpse of his relation to his brothers; Ezekiel's wheels; Paul's sense of the need of Macedonia. All were day or night dreams.

Science has never been able to prove that the human mind ever rests. Some great minds work all night, and marvels have been catalogued to prove that glimpses of light, too dazzling for daytime, sometimes visit during sleeping hours.

I question most dreams I have and yet I don't doubt that God, who employs sunsets and rainbows as teachers, who speaks through mountain silences and the lips of little children, may also make use of what we call "dreams."

Dreaming is good, but don't lose your dream as did Demas. There's no such word as "impossible" in the vocabulary of dreams. The world scoffed at David Livingstone and his dream for Africa. The Jews scoffed at Jesus and His glorious dream for men. Whatever else one may do without, he can by no means do without his dream.

Always the dream first—always the dream. And so also with being a Christian; no one can be one until God has given him a sunrise in his soul. The first thing Jesus did for Peter and Zacchaeus and the woman at the well was to share His dream with them. And the immortal ministry of a converted Pharisee was simply the fulfillment of a certain dream God gave him on the Damascus road.

So, too, Demas had his dream. He lived it out in human terms, for a season. Paul refers to Demas twice as he writes from his cell in a Roman prison, and refers to him affectionately. He was dear to his spiritual father, Paul. But, oh, the dreams that fade with the advent of day.

Friends, I am thinking of you and your dreams. I want to remind you of the wonder of them, and of the tragedy of losing them. God sent you a great moment. He gave you a dream of what you might be and do—don't lose it! Demas lost his, for Paul said, "Demas has deserted me."

Demas was the man who forgot his dream. He got a transfer from Paul to others, from God to the world. Love did it—misplaced love. Love weaves crowns of thorns as well as of roses. Too many of us love the wrong thing, as did Demas. He misplaced his love when he lost his dream. He loved the present world and forgot his dream. Worldliness slipped in.

Keep your dream, in your thinking and in your actions. Hold fast to your ideals. Be sure you have a dream, a vision, and then permit nothing to intrude, for when worldliness once gains admittance, the dream is spoiled. Then He who writes our scores makes this notation: "This once beloved follower has forsaken me, having loved the present world."

(Excerpted from a message by Virgil Reed, given on January 16, 1944.)

Naomi Responds

Dreams grow holy put in action.

Adelaide Anne Procter

Demas lost his dream. He deserted the vision, the mission, the highest, the best. How could that happen? We nod, and realize it happens all too often. It happens to others, it happens to us.

We lose our dream of a happy marriage, a family raised to serve the Lord, a commitment to honesty, integrity, influence. We lose the dream of a life of serving others with devotion, loyalty, and love—or the dream of reaching out to a dying, hurting, and hopeless world.

Lost dreams! Broken dreams! But then, we're encouraged again, another chance, to dream again. "To Dream the Impossible Dream" echoes in our hearts when we hear the call of God, and we view a hurting world! We stop and realize He empowers, He indwells, He purposes, and He accomplishes.

Consider the stories of Henrietta and Agnes, who dared to dream seemingly impossible dreams. Born in obscurity, on opposite sides of the world, they pursued dreams that were destined to impact the 20th century like few others had. Today, long after their deaths, the legacy they left continues to bear rich fruit around the world.

Henrietta was born in 1890 in Fargo, North Dakota, and Agnes in 1910, in ancient Macedonia—two different worlds. Yet, there are amazing similarities in their lives. Neither ever married and, as young adults, each began a career as a high school teacher. And each, at age 38, took the first step toward fulfilling her God-given dream.

Even as a teenager, Henrietta's dream, of a career in the field of Christian education, began to take shape. After graduating from the University of Minnesota, and teaching high school in Minneapolis for 13 years, she felt God leading her to California, where she became Director of Christian Education at the First Presbyterian Church of Hollywood. During 35 years in that post, she also taught Sunday School classes for college students, more than 400 of whom went on to full-time Christian ministry all around the world.

Her students included Bill Bright, the founder of Campus Crusade for Christ, and Dick Halverson, a pastor and later Chaplain of the U.S. Senate. A woman of great vision, Henrietta also founded Gospel Light Publications, Forest Home Christian Conference Center, and Gospel Literature International. Following her death in 1963, Bill Bright wrote: "Dr. Henrietta Mears was truly one of the great women of the twentieth century and one of the greatest influences of my life."

Halfway around the world, Agnes had become a nun and was teaching at St. Mary's High School in Calcutta, India when she decided to pursue her dream. With permission from her superiors, she left the convent school to devote her life to working among the poorest of the poor in the Calcutta slums—beggars and children dying in the streets, dirty, unwanted, and ignored. So Agnes Bojaxhiu, who as a nun had become Mother Teresa, begin a ministry she would continue and expand until her death in 1997.

For nearly a half-century, Mother Teresa gave unselfish, serving benevolence. She never forsook her dream. Rather, she perpetuated it, starting homes for the poor, the dying, the leprosy laden, the unfortunate throughout the entire world. A champion of the unwanted, the unborn, the unloved, she traveled the world well into her 80s, with a challenge to the "haves for the have nots." The Missionaries of Charity, which she founded, now has more than one million co-workers, carrying on her labor of love in over 40 countries.

As an elderly lady, stooped with arthritis, and barely 4'9" tall, Mother Teresa was asked how she felt being so bowed by her disease. Her response was classic: "It is not a problem, because I just get closer and closer to those I love."

She died with just five possessions: two robes, sandals, a bowl, and a Bible. But she died with a wealth of dreams realized, a Nobel Peace Prize, and assuredly a welcome home from her Heavenly Father, saying, "Well done, good and faithful servant."

Unlike Demas, Henrietta and Agnes never lost their dreams. They dared to dream big dreams, trusting God to make them come true. The lesson for all of us is this: as long as we remain faithful to them, our God-centered dreams can continue to influence lives long after He has called us home—and that's the greatest lesson of all.

Chapter
5
The Power
of Forgiveness

"Blessed is he whose transgressions are forgiven, whose sins are covered. Blessed is the man whose sin the Lord does not count against him and in whose spirit is no deceit…Then I acknowledged my sin to you and did not cover up my iniquity. I said, 'I will confess my transgressions to the Lord'—and you forgave the guilt of my sin."

Psalm 32:1, 2, 5

If your sins and mine are only forgiven by God as we forgive those who trespass against us, what condition is our soul in this morning?

(Virgil Reed)

As I read my father's words of faith in our Heavenly Father's forgiveness, I'm overwhelmed with the blessed realization of a legacy of forgiveness!

(Naomi Reed Rhode)

**He that cannot forgive others breaks the bridge over
which he himself must pass if he would ever reach
heaven; for every one has need to be forgiven.**

George Herbert

F ather, forgive them for they know not what they do," prayed
Christ on the cross. In our Lord's Prayer, we have that often
repeated and little thought of phrase, "as we forgive those who
trespass against us." What a dangerous part of that wonderful prayer.
If your sins and mine are only forgiven by God as we forgive those
who trespass against us, what condition is our soul in this morning?

Just what is sin? It's murder, drunkenness or robbery. But before
anyone here endeavors to avoid the need of forgiveness, let's add to
that list the sins of temperament, of sullenness, of vindictiveness, of
bad temper. Then, where do we stand, if not in need of the forgiveness of our Father?

The sin of neglect needs forgiveness. The things we leave undone
often count as sins. It may be the letter we didn't write, the words we
didn't speak, the opportunity we didn't take to speak for Christ.

Once there was a man who had one talent, which he hid in his
napkin. What did he do? That was the trouble—he didn't do anything. He missed his opportunity and committed the sin of omission.

The priest and the Levite who left the victim on the road wounded and about to die, what did they do? They did nothing but pass by
on the other side. Does our need of forgiveness point to our neglect
of some sin-laden neighbor or acquaintance?

There's a commonly mistaken idea about forgiveness. Many people believe it's very easy to forgive sin. But it's not true. It's hard to
forgive sins. Pardon has been often presented as an easy gospel. No!
It's hard to forgive sins, hard for us against our neighbor, and hard for
Christ. "Which is easier," said Jesus, "to say thy sins are forgiven
thee, or to say arise and walk?" He says it's easier for a palsied man
to walk than to say, "Thy sins are forgiven thee."

When you hear someone talking lightly about sin and forgiveness,
you can be sure he's not forgiving sin—he's condoning it. To be gracious and tolerant about sin is not forgiveness, but moral looseness.
Remember that sin does matter. It matters tremendously. To condone
sin is easy—to forgive sin is hard.

Jesus so loved the poor victim on the road left wounded and

stripped that he was hard on the priest and the Levite. Christ has a plumb line that reaches to the very bottom of sin. He takes sin seriously. Nobody ever hated sin as much as did Christ, and yet He taught forgiveness. That's the miracle. When we're forgiven of a sin, it's another miracle performed in us.

Forgiveness does only one thing. It doesn't take away the fact or the memory of sin. Neither does it take away the consequences of sin. But it does reestablish the personal relationships that have been broken by sin, and makes them deeper and sweeter.

The cross on Calvary cost a great price. When the Gospel invites us to forgiveness, it never invites us to a lighthearted place where sin is condoned. It calls us to a cross. For whether it's a mother forgiving a son, or God forgiving us, a cross is always at the center of it, and it's never easy.

Psychiatrists tell us that most cases of mental derangement are due to a sense of guilt resulting from a lack of forgiveness. And so this morning, friends, as we consider this very serious topic of forgiveness, let each of us go down into that secret place, unlock that hidden door, take out that unforgiven sin and, for our soul's sake, get rid of it.

But there's only one way to do that and that way is the way of the Cross—of penitence, confession, restitution, pardon. May He who is mighty to save be merciful to us and forgive us, that we may be able to say with the Psalmist, "As far as the east is from the west, so far have my sins been removed from me."

(Excerpted from a message by Virgil Reed, given on January 14, 1940.)

Naomi Responds

Our unwillingness to forgive when we've been deeply hurt breeds self-pity and bitterness. If you will learn and experience God's love and forgiveness through Jesus, you will have no problem in forgiving anyone for anything.

Charlie "Tremendous" Jones

As I sit in the quiet of my home and read my father's words of faith in our Heavenly Father's forgiveness, I'm overwhelmed with the blessed realization of a legacy of forgiveness. I grew up knowing my Dad had experienced His Heavenly Father's forgiveness, through Christ on the cross, for him. It was not an easy sacrifice, but a promised substitution of His blood, His life, for my father's life, his sin—and a propitiation for my sin, past, present, and future.

What incredible freedom, through forgiveness, that provides for those of us who believe in Jesus, and His sacrifice for us. Do we really grasp the meaning, the realization? We're free! We're forgiven. What an incredible mandate for us, then, *to forgive others as He has forgiven us!* Doesn't that cause you to pause "in awe?" And then, what does it do for me, when I forgive another for a wrong against me?

Some years ago, a dear friend of mine died in her early 40s of breast cancer, leaving a wonderful husband and family. She wasn't a believer when diagnosed, but quickly turned to the Lord in a radiant faith, and spent the remaining four years of her life in total peace, sharing His love and forgiveness.

Early in her new spiritual journey, overwhelmed with her own forgiveness, she made a list of all those she needed to forgive. She prayerfully and systematically went about forgiving the wrongs she held tightly within her.

With many of them, she spoke directly; for others, she wrote letters of forgiveness. For all of them, she made a lifelong impact in freeing, not only herself from the bondage of unforgiveness, but them from their bondage too.

She shared with me a painfully poignant letter she sent to the physician who had failed to detect the lump in her breast, on the x-ray, 10 years prior to her diagnosis. In that letter, she forgave him, acknowledged his humanness, and lack of intent, and asked him to stop in and see her in the hospital, where they shared a tearful reunion.

Not only was it powerful closure for my friend Deb, but an affirmation and empowerment for the future medical practice of that doctor.

I asked several people in my life for a definition of forgiveness. My sister-in-law Carol said, "Forgiveness is my choice to personally bear the consequences of your choice and never again hold you responsible for what you did to hurt me."

My then 11-year-old grandson Titus said, "Forgiveness is when you don't hold something against another person in your heart. It's a very good thing to do."

Another 11-year old grandson, Quinlan, said, "Forgiveness is something people are born without and most people never get. And, that's sad, because God wants us all to have it."

My granddaughter Kylin, age 9, said, "Forgiveness is to forgive someone for a bad thing they did, and then forget about it. It doesn't matter, anymore. Go on and be friends with them."

What a marvelous insight into God's forgiveness, mirrored in a child's response: "It doesn't matter, anymore. Go on and be friends with them."

That is exactly what the Lord offers us in the free gift of salvation! Certainly it isn't a 'license to sin,' but rather an overwhelming realization of gratitude for the debt we owed, which He paid. His blood shed for us paid for our sins past, present and future, when we put our trust and faith in His substitutionary death on the cross.

What an incredible model for our lives—to forgive as we have been forgiven.

So may it be for you, and for me: forgiving others, as Christ has forgiven us.

Chapter
6
Fear and Worry

"Yea, though I walk through the valley of the shadow of death, I shall fear no evil…"

Psalm 23:4

The mind is its own place and can make a heaven of hell or a hell of heaven.

(Virgil Reed)

We can have victory now over the daily fear and worry of trivial and real challenges, because of Christ's indwelling peace.

(Naomi Reed Rhode)

Anxiety does not empty tomorrow of its sorrows but only empties today of its strength.

Charles H. Spurgeon

The world, everybody, science, literature, art, government, society and religion are in a hot, mad, anxious search for but one thing—happiness. Where is happiness to be found? And where is the place of peace? Within! But peace and happiness are so close to the searchers that few find them, because our fears crowd them out. The mind is its own place and can make a heaven of hell or a hell of heaven.

What causes us to fear? First, there are physical causes: certain kinds of food (raw oysters, for example); our appearance (overweight, wrinkles, hair loss, etc.)

Second, there are ethical causes, which bring guilt, another name for fear. Secret sin, failure to do our duty, etc. bring guilt. Third, there are mental causes, brought on by ignorance, insecurities, overactive imaginations, negative and pessimistic thoughts.

Last, there are spiritual causes: a lack of faith and a loss of trust in God.

Fear causes us to focus on the very evils we fear. Job said: "The thing I greatly fear has come upon me." Let a dog sense that you're afraid and you're inviting an attack.

Fear is a dragon we must trample underfoot. We load up with so many needless worries, fears enough to weigh us down and hinder us from running the Christian race well.

Do we transmit and scatter worry and fear? Should we, like someone infected with a highly contagious disease, be segregated from others?

"As a man thinketh, so is he." We are just as big, or as good, or as kind, or as mean, as we think we are. Bear in mind the example of King David, who declared: "Yea, though I walk through the valley of the shadow of death, I shall fear no evil" (Psalm 23:4).

Bear in mind God's promises throughout Scripture:

- "Fear not, I am thy shield." (Genesis 15:4)
- "Fear not, I am with thee" (Isaiah 41:10)
- "Fear not, I have redeemed thee" (Isaiah 43:1)

- "Fear not, little flock, for it is the Father's good will to give thee the kingdom" (Luke 12:32)
- "Fear none of these things" (Revelation 2:10)

Walking along the road where we meet worry and fear daily, they need not be stumbling blocks. When fears and worries present themselves, pray, sing a song, recite a poem or verse of Scripture. Dismiss those fearful thoughts by replacing them with more positive and uplifting ones.

(Excerpted from a message by Virgil Reed, given on January 9, 1944.)

Naomi Responds

Worry is spiritual nearsightedness, a fumbling way of looking at little things, and of magnifying their value.

Anna Robertson Brown

9-11!! Those numbers will never again mean the same as they once did. For years, 911 has been the accepted number sequence for help, for emergencies, for assurance. And then the unthinkable happened. America was attacked within our very own borders.

We'll always remember where we were on that day. We'll always remember the disbelief, staring at our television sets for hours and the replay of those proud Twin Towers tumbling down, enveloped in clouds of smoke and dust.

We'll always remember the families trudging the streets of New York looking for loved ones, and the stark disbelief of fellow workers at the Pentagon.

We'll always remember the heroes—firefighters, police, health workers, and civilians on an airplane, aborting the terrible plan of terrorists to strike our nation's Capitol.

Fear! Worry! More fear, more worry—a world swirling with the infiltration of terrorists in our cities, our communities, our airplanes, our schools and businesses.

Only now do we perhaps truly personalize what much of the rest of the world has experienced in one way or another for centuries— centuries of man's inequity and hatred against our fellow man.

But wait! What about the Gospel, the Good News? What is its echo in the years before Christ's birth, the years of His presence on earth, and His presence now in our hearts? David speaks it to our hearts in the Psalms, "Even though I walk through the valley of the shadow of death, I will fear no evil, for you are with me" (Psalm 23:4). "The Lord is my strength and my shield" (Psalm 28:7).

Perhaps in eternity we'll know of all the millions of times these passages have been repeated, as surgeries have been faced, death's dark door has creaked open, and towers have tumbled down.

Fear and worry probably cause more disease, and certainly "dis-ease" than any other factors. The emotional response in suppressing our immune systems, causing us to make poor choices, and freezing us in the tight hold of fear's grip, takes a dangerous toll on our mortality, and our daily purpose in life.

We "awfulize," and we realize. We project and we anticipate. And yet, and yet—this is the very thing Christ came to relieve. He promises His peace and relief, though the storms rage.

Scripture promises, sadly, that there will always be wars and rumors of war. Man's hatred toward man will not be done away with until Satan himself is finally conquered.

But, as has so often been said, "We know the end of the story, and we win!" We win because of what Jesus did on the cross. Death was conquered. His redemptive plan was realized! And we can have victory now over the daily fear and worry of trivial and real challenges because of Christ's indwelling peace.

What then is the real sequence of numbers for help and assurance? We find it in the Gospel of John, when Jesus said to His disciples: "Peace I leave with you; my peace I give you. I do not give to you as the world gives. Do not let your hearts be troubled and do not be afraid" (John 14:27)

His peace is in spite of, not instead of—and is as certain today as when He first spoke those words 2,000 years ago!

Thank you, Lord Jesus, that your indwelling Spirit is the only protection and the 'always' protection from fear and worry we will ever need.

Chapter
7

Think on
These Things

"Finally Brethren, whatsoever things are true; whatsoever things are honest; whatsoever things are just; whatsoever things are pure; whatsoever things are lovely; whatsoever things are of good report; if there be any virtue and if there be any praise, think on these things."

Philippians 4:8

I've come that I might give you something whole-some by which you might live better this week then you otherwise would have.

(Virgil Reed)

We're shaped and molded by the books, the thoughts, the Word of God, that we dwell on daily.

(Naomi Reed Rhode)

Good thoughts are blessed guests, and should be heartily welcomed, well-fed and much sought after.

Charles H. Spurgeon

It has wisely been stated that if you sow a thought you will reap an act; if you sow an act, you will reap a habit; if you sow a habit, you will reap a destiny. What you think is eventually what you become. I'm wondering what you've been thinking this past week, because what you've been thinking determines what you've been.

Perhaps the Apostle Paul, next to Jesus, was the most outstanding example for Christians to follow. As I think of Paul, I recall that marvelous testimony he so often gave: "I know whom I have believed and I am persuaded that He is able to keep that which I have committed unto him against that day."

Paul made another statement, which I should like to make before you this afternoon, because I've come that I might give you something wholesome by which you might live better this week then you otherwise would have.

Paul said, " I am determined to know nothing among you, save Jesus Christ and Him crucified." And this is my lesson at this Vesper hour this afternoon, "To know nothing among you, save Jesus Christ and Him crucified."

But to get back to the text, "Whatsoever things are true, think on these things." And if you think on these things, you will talk about them. So let us be very sure that a report we have heard about someone is absolutely true. Let's also be sure it bears repeating even if it is true. It may do damage to repeat it. But if a report is untrue and repeated, how great is the trouble that can be brewed.

"Whatsoever things are honest, think on these things." I'm wondering if you and I are honest with God. I'm wondering if we're absolutely honest with ourselves. It has been said that honesty by far is the best policy. Paul says, "If you can think on honest things, the God of peace will be with you to be your guide and comfort."

He tells us to think pure thoughts. Paul says, "Let us clean the rubbish out of our minds and think only those things that are pure. Think on those things that are beautiful, amiable, and delightful and worthy for a Christian to think of, but not the slander and backbiting, the discouraging reports and the gossip."

The great Queen Victoria was at one time asked to what she

attributed her long and successful reign. She replied, "I chose a motto that was to guide me through life, and that motto is a passage of Scripture."

I'm going to share that passage with you this afternoon and, even though you may have trouble finding other passages of Scripture, I'm sure you'll always be able to find this one whenever you want it. It consists of the first four words, of the first verse, of the first chapter, of the first book of the Bible: "In the beginning God."

When she was asked to explain, she said, " In the morning of each day I would take things to God in prayer. At the beginning of every undertaking, I considered what his plans would be for the case."

I'm wondering if that would be a splendid motto for you and me to follow tomorrow, the next week, and all through life—in the beginning of every day, to take God into consideration and to think His thoughts.

(Excerpted from a message by Virgil Reed at a YWCA Vesper Service, Fargo, N.D., March 1942)

Naomi Responds

**You are today where your thoughts have brought you;
you will be tomorrow where your thoughts take you.**

James Allen

Glance back for a moment on the passage from Philippians 4:8, the "whatsoever passage." What a list! What a standard of beauty, excellence, health, wellness, abundance!

How we limit our potential by opting for the puny thoughts, the unworthy thoughts, the evil thoughts, the envious thoughts, the vain thoughts, rather than the God-glorifying reality of "My Utmost for His Highest."

How, why, does this happen?

I remember Mother and Dad often saying to me, "You can only give out what you have taken in." In other words, you can only become what the input (the ingredients of your life) has been. Our education, music, reading, poetry, people, places, positions, experiences all play a part in shaping the person we become.

But, the choices are ours, from the smorgasbord of God's goodness and grace to Satan's platter of prattle, and worthless ingredients.

For years, I was wary of a mandate for a daily "quiet time" with the Lord. Certainly the legalistic reason for this listening/learning time alone with God is invalid. But I've found that when I seclude myself, often on my prayer/praise patio, and worship Him, first thing in the morning, my mind and my heart overflow with His love, His message, His grace.

As I choose to 'think on these things,' I'm almost always spurred on to some action for the day, some meditation to ponder in my heart and mind, some comfort or solace for a problem or heartache.

My good friend, Charlie 'Tremendous' Jones, says, "You are the same today as you'll be in five years except for two things: the people you meet and the books you read." His voracious love of reading, of sharing the written word audibly with others, is a lifestyle habit that truly is revolutionary for worthy living. His passion for reading has increased my choice of reading tremendously! It motivated me, over the past decade, to make a list of all my reading each year. How I wish I had done that my entire life.

We're shaped and molded by the books, the thoughts, the Word of God, that we dwell on daily.

With the information explosion in our society, and Internet access, the amount of information available is absolutely mind-boggling. It's impossible to know it all, read it all, or keep up with it all. It behooves us more and more to selectively choose what we'll spend our time doing, what we'll read, watch on TV, see on the Internet or in entertainment venues, and listen to on radio/CDs.

As a young girl, I remember my parents' seemingly narrow view on what movies I could see. I also remember my mother telling me about something she had seen that she'd have given almost anything to be able to erase from her mind. She told me how this 'thing' would pop up in her dreams and her thoughts, and that it was now her privilege to make sure her parent filter for me was one of goodness and worth.

Truly her example was lived out, as I witnessed both my parents "thinking on things that were true, honest, just, pure, lovely, and of good report." What an awesome legacy of influence!

Chapter
8
From Vision
to Service

"About eight days after Jesus said this, he took Peter, John and James with him and went up onto a mountain to pray. As he was praying, the appearance of his face changed, and his clothes became as bright as a flash of lightning. Two men, Moses and Elijah, appeared in glorious splendor, talking with Jesus...As the men were leaving Jesus, Peter said to him, 'Master, it is good for us to be here. Let us put up three shelters—one for you, one for Moses and one for Elijah."'...While he was speaking, a cloud appeared and enveloped them, and they were afraid as they entered the cloud. A voice came from the cloud, saying, 'This is my Son, whom I have chosen; listen to him.'"

Luke 9:28-35

We must come down from the mountain in order to be of service.

(Virgil Reed)

Be changed, so that as you return to the valley, you'll be eager to turn the vision you've had of Him into service for Him.

(Naomi Reed Rhode)

The way up is down. The way to honor our Lord and Savior is to serve. There is always room for one more servant.

Francis M. Cosgrove, Jr.

The three disciples Jesus took with him to the mountain were his Inner Circle: Peter, who would become the prince of the apostles; John, the beloved; and James, who would be the first apostle to be martyred. It was to be a mountaintop experience for all of them.

As Jesus prayed, something happened to him, as "the appearance of his face changed." Does anything happen when we pray? How long has it been since your countenance was changed because you had prayed?

When Moses and Elijah appeared, I wonder if the three disciples remembered that Jesus had once said: "I have come to fulfill the law and the prophets." They knew of Moses as the lawgiver and Elijah as the prophet, and now they could see them talking with Jesus, the Son of Man, in all his glory.

Before Moses and Elijah disappeared, Peter suggested putting up shelters for them. Was his suggestion a foolish one? Was he, in his impetuous way, like that class of people who, when they don't know what to say, say it anyway? Was he being honest, or did he just want to stay and enjoy the mountaintop experience? Was he trying to escape the coming events in Jerusalem, of which Jesus had warned him? He still couldn't see the need for Jesus to go to his destruction in Jerusalem.

Perhaps Peter failed to realize that visions are calls to action and, in this case, to meet the needs of the crowd of people waiting for Jesus at the foot of the mountain.

Then the cloud came and covered them, and the disciples were afraid. Yet it was only a cloud, a shadow, and shadows can't harm us. As Christians, there is no need to be afraid. Though we walk through the valley of the shadow of death, it's only a shadow.

We have the privilege of going to the mountaintop at will. There we can meet quietly with our God, draw nearer to him and enjoy his presence. But then we must come down from the mountain so that others may catch that to which we've been exposed. We must come down from the mountain in order to be of service, to spread the message of the Gospel, to heal the sick and bind up wounded hearts, to feed his sheep and his lambs, and to do the Lord's will.

A man came to church late on Sunday morning, so late in fact that, as he arrived, the sermon had been completed and the people were leaving. "Is it all done?" he asked. "No," said one of the congregation. "It has only been *said*. We are just starting out now to *do* it."

Now, let us all go out from this place to do the will of our Father. And let us never neglect to do the little things, for thereby we may be doing great things for the Master.

(Excerpted from a message by Virgil Reed, Baker, Minn., March 29, 1942)

Naomi Responds

**God is the source of love; Christ is the proof of love;
Service is the expression of love.**

Henrietta C. Mears

Whenever I read these words of my Dad's, my mind fills with the privilege and memory of mountaintop experiences.

I remember camp experiences as a child and young adult. In fact, I met my husband, Jim at a Christian camp when I was just 12 years old, and he was 14.

I remember the feeling of arriving at camp, not knowing many of the kids, wondering what my place would be in the milling throngs of unknown campers, concepts, activities. I remember the first few days of 'fitting in,' and learning the ropes. And I remember the gradual transition to the feeling of belonging, fun, and mountain climbing.

And then—the last evening celebration. Laughter, reminiscing, skits, and the 'mountaintop experience' of the closing campfire.

Those 'mountaintop experiences' set precedents that I've sought and caught many times over throughout life—retreats, study groups, cadres of professional colleagues, and intimate times with close circles of friends or family.

I'm privileged to share those special 'mountaintop' times with my *Chaber* sisters, five dear Phoenix friends I've met with regularly over the past two decades. (*Chaber* is a Hebrew word meaning "bound together by cords of love.")

Other 'mountaintop' times for me include: a three-day annual retreat with my Summit Sisters, four women from around the country who are also professional speakers; a Bible Study group in our home through many years—sharing that's tender and rich; and, of course, my family, who care, love, share, and bless my heart.

As all-important as these relationships are to me, there's another 'mountaintop experience' that must be of paramount importance in my life and yours, for it's there we meet with our Savior and Lord. He came to die, so that He could come to dwell—to dwell in you and me.

His name is Jesus. He is the Son of God. He was born of a virgin, lived in sandals, walking dusty roads, identifying with our world. He died because of us, because of my sin and yours. He died so that we might find the way to the Father, the Holy God of the Universe. He was resurrected and ascended to the Father so that we might receive His Holy Spirit into our lives, to sustain and guide us along the roads we walk each day.

We long for these mountaintop experiences! We need the reenergizing power of relationships, experiences, new vision. But it can also be a daily, life-changing experience amidst the chaos of reality!

I have a special place, a special "mountaintop"—a prayer and praise patio. It's always available to me, always waiting. As I rise early in the morning, with my coffee, my Oswald Chambers' *My Utmost For His Highest*, my Bible, and other reading, I meet my Lord on that mountaintop, where He lifts my load, lightens my spirit, encourages my heart, and increases my vision for the service He has for me each day.

When we're traveling, I take my "prayer and praise patio" with me. It's totally portable: a Palm Pilot in hand, with Bible and books downloaded, a quick search for a quiet lobby, a park bench, or a hotel room solace provides—Voila!—a mountaintop! And He meets me there.

Is it simply a tradition? A requisite? A responsibility? A mandate for discipleship? Certainly studying God's Word is an integral part of a believer's life. But it's far more than that! It's my utmost privilege—to hear the Father's voice as he reminds me daily, "This is my Son, whom I have chosen; listen to Him."

My journals record the power of those times, the prayer requests, the pages of praise, the insight and 'vision,' and mostly the worship and awe of the Creator of the Earth, meeting me, Naomi, on a mountaintop to give daily vision and guidance.

And He always has time to meet you there too! The appointment is a 'standing one' in His book! Be there! Let Him fill you with His love! Be changed, so that as you return to the valley, you'll be eager to turn the vision you've had of Him into service for Him.

Chapter

9

Satellites

"The heavens declare the glory of God; the skies proclaim the work of his hands."

Psalm 19:1

We're all called to be satellites, revolving around the great God whom we worship, borrowing all our beams from the Sun of Righteousness.

(Virgil Reed)

It may often be inadvertent, yet we're consistently and powerfully impacting those with whom we come in contact.

(Naomi Reed Rhode)

There are two ways of spreading light: to be the candle, or the mirror that reflects it.

Edith Wharton

Who among us hasn't marveled at the greatness of our Creator God, as we've studied and gazed upon the wonder of the starry sky? As we pursue the study of the science of the universe, and the magnitude of the solar system and the myriad of other systems equally vast, we may look at ourselves and ask: "How big am I, anyway?"

Sometimes we feel terribly important, in our homes, in our school systems, in our community. We're sometimes sure the world couldn't endure for long without our contributions. So, let us, for a moment, reflect on the thought: "How big am I, after all?"

Let's compare ourselves to the size of this building we're in, or to the size of our city, and we begin to shrink in size. Then, if we go further and think of the county, the state, the nation, the continent in which we live, and then of the world itself, we realize we're not so large or important after all.

But we can't even stop with the world, for it's only a tiny part of our solar system. And that system, with its many planets and satellites, is only one of hundreds of similar systems. As we try to see ourselves in comparison to the vastness of God's creation, we fade into nothingness.

And yet, each of us is extremely important for, within each of us, there has been planted an immortal soul. We are the children of a Heavenly King.

The psalmist, with much wisdom, wrote: "When I consider the work of Thy hands, the sun and moon which Thou hast ordained, what is man that Thou art mindful of him?" (Psalm 8:3-4)

Today, I wish to speak to you on the subject of "Satellites." A satellite hangs onto, and attends or follows, a larger planet in its course. The planet shines, as does our sun, while the satellite absorbs light. If a satellite ever shines, it does so by reflected light only. The moon is a satellite of the earth, and when it shines, it is only reflecting the light of the sun.

I've been describing satellites that inhabit the heavens, but we also have satellites here on earth—not globes or planets, but people.

A person who's a satellite revolves unceasingly around other lives. Such souls shine by reflected light only.

We can choose what kind of satellites we'll be, whether stumbling blocks or steppingstones. Or we can choose, as some do, to be planets, so absorbed with self that we reflect no light at all.

As faithful Christians, we're all called to be satellites, revolving around the great God whom we worship, borrowing all our beams from the Sun of Righteousness. We revolve around a life which was laid down for our lives. If any of us glows, it's by reflection only. God has appointed us to shine by reflecting His glory and majesty; therefore, we must keep our faces bright. Can others tell by the glow on your face that you are God's satellite?

(Excerpted from a message by Virgil Reed, Fargo, North Dakota, February 13, 1944)

Naomi Responds

**There are two ways of spreading light: to be the candle,
or the mirror that reflects it.**

Edith Wharton

Jesus told His disciples: "You are the light of the world…let your light shine before men, that they may see your good deeds and praise your Father in heaven" (Matthew 5:14, 16).

There is a whole association of people who are called 'Sky Watchers.' There are people who spend their time being 'Cloud Watchers,' 'Tornado Watchers/Chasers,' 'Tide (ocean) Watchers,' 'Bird Watchers,' 'Whale Watchers,' etc.

But, all of us, perhaps without realizing it, are perpetual 'People Watchers.' From the time children are newborns, they listen, watch, and mimic those who surround them, who are in their world.

Often we're dismayed as we experience children who scream, throw tantrums, swear, hit, or bully in public places. We usually don't have to wonder where this behavior initiated. Whether it be from a home environment, neighborhood, or from the media, most of what's portrayed is mimicked from the environment of experience.

In radiant contrast, we watch children in homes where education, values, virtue and love are exhibited. These children live out these disciplines with grace and ease.

The true story is told of a tragic car accident in which the parents of two small sons were killed. The grandparents and an aunt and uncle literally flipped a coin for which child they would take and raise.

The grandparents took the five-year-old into their home. As educators, they had filled every room, even the kitchen, with books. Their grandson had educational opportunities, discipline, caring, learning and values as an integral part of his daily experience.

The aunt and uncle took the six-year-old into their home, where addictive behavior, drugs, bad language and lack of discipline were the standard lifestyle.

Years passed. The reflection of the environment in which they'd been raised was absorbed into the "satellite lives" of these two precious children. The first one became president of a large university on the East Coast. The older one, from the drug-ravished home, went to prison for life for dealing and using drugs.

Many of us who are believers have no idea of the power of the light that shines in and through us on a regular basis, giving hope where there is no hope—giving light in abject darkness, and bringing purpose to a hurting world. It may often be inadvertent, yet we're consistently and powerfully impacting those with whom we come in contact.

As we "let our light shine," we can be reflectors, satellites, of that one true Light, Jesus Himself, to a dark and hurting world.

Chapter
10
A Winsome Invitation

"Come unto me, ye that are labor and are heavy laden, and I will give you rest."

Matthew 11:28

All toilers, all burden bearers, are included in this invitation. And I have an idea that includes just about all of us.

(Virgil Reed)

It's an invitation to come and see His grace, His mercy, His life given for us. But, also, the invitation is to come and to share His yoke.

(Naomi Reed Rhode)

The heart of man is restless until it finds its rest in Thee.

Saint Augustine

My business with you in these words is very simple. I'm here as an invitation bearer. It's not my invitation, but another's. I'm here to deliver it as winsomely as I can. You decide if the invitation is addressed to you personally.

Listen to the invitation and see if it calls your name: "Come unto me ye that labor and are heavy laden, and I will give you rest. Take my yoke upon you, and learn of me, for I am meek and lowly in heart: and ye shall find rest unto your souls. For my yoke is easy and my burden is light."

This invitation from Jesus is extended to two groups. The first is to laborers. "Come unto me all ye that labor." Labor is more than work. Work is a privilege. Labor is work carried on at the price of weariness and pain, work that has become agony, work that has degenerated into toil. It's being on the same old treadmill, day after day.

To struggle and labor and toil in a cause and see it fail is disheartening. It brings agony of body, or soul, or mind. If you're experiencing "labor," then yours is one of the names Jesus is calling.

The second group Jesus invites is "the burdened"—"the heavy laden." Oh, how many of us carry a burden even our friends know nothing about? Then, this invitation is for you. It may be a burden of anxiety, fear, lack of income, ill health, pain, sin, sorrow, disappointment, or a death. You are acquainted with tears because of your burdens.

All toilers, all burden bearers, are included in this invitation. And I have an idea that includes just about all of us.

What does Jesus invite us to do?—To "Come unto me." He could never see a crowd without holding his hands out to them as a mother to a frightened child. Jesus stills gives that invitation and still means it.

He also says, "Take my yoke"—accept my yoke and my authority – take the yoke I bear. "Come unto me" calls for a decision (enlistment). "Take my yoke" calls for a dedicated life.

Jesus bore a yoke—the yoke of complete surrender to God's will.

He said; "I came not to do mine own will, but the will of Him who sent me."

We are invited to come and to take His yoke. Jesus does not force a yoke upon us.

He invites us. But, whether we accept or reject His invitation, we still will bear a yoke—His or another—the yoke of Christ or the yoke of sin.

Why bear his yoke? He tells us His yoke is easy and the burden is light. That seems strange, because it cost him everything. He became "a man of sorrows and acquainted with grief." His yoke cost Him Gethsemane and Calvary and the grave. It led Him to cry, "My God, My God, why hast Thou forsaken me?"

Yet He says His yoke is easy and light, resulting in a radiant and joyful life. In praying for His disciples before He went to the cross, He prayed that they might have His joy fulfilled in themselves.

His yoke is easy because it is born from a great motive. A heavy yoke? Yes, but light because of the motive. Jesus fits our yoke and will make it just right. Let's carry His load with Him.

(Excerpted from a message by Virgil Reed in Hawley, Minnesota, date unknown.)

Naomi Responds

**In the restless sea of human passions, Christ
stands steadfast and calm, ready to welcome all
who will turn to Him.**

Billy Graham

The "Come and See Class" was the name of the adult Sunday School class my father taught in Fargo, North Dakota for many years. As a child, I was always intrigued by that name. "Come and See" what? Who? Why?

And then, as a young Christian, the Scriptures revealed the answer to my questions. "Come and See" was the echo of Christ's invitation—indeed a "winsome invitation" to come to Him. It's an invitation to come and see His grace, His mercy, His life given for us. But, also, the invitation is to come and to share His yoke.

Most of us have seen pictures of oxen plowing the hard earth as a team, sharing a yoke, pulling together to prepare the field for the seed which will grow and bear fruit.

Christ uses this agricultural picture of heavy loads, cares shared and burdens lightened. He promises to not only share our load, but that His yoke is easy and His burden is light.

When we read the stories of those who have sacrificed much for their faith, even to be martyred for identification with Jesus, it's hard to affirm that His burden is light. And, yet, as we study the seeming sacrifices of these lives, we find that obviously they've shared in His life's purpose with light hearts, and eyes gleaming with the purpose of glorifying Him.

We may never be called personally to such life experiences. But we are invited to come—to come and see—to come and share, and to come with our labors and our burdens, laying them at His feet.

What a winsome partnership Christ promises. When we "come and see," we inevitably "go and be" His people in a world filled with heavy burdens and intense labors.

When you hear that "winsome invitation," what happens in your soul? Do you believe it? Do you run, not walk, to respond? Do you come into His arms, knowing He knew before you got there? Do you know that His wisdom is profound, beyond your understanding?

Do you know Jesus cares more than you're able to comprehend? And, do you know, do I know, that no one can take away this "winsome invitation," whether we're in the deepest darkness of our soul's night, or the brilliant daybreak of the happiest day of our lives?

Have you responded to this "winsome invitation"? If not, "come and see."

Chapter
11
Shining Lights?
Or Secret Agents?

"You are the light of the world...Let your light so shine before men that they may see your good works and glorify your Father which is in Heaven."

Matthew 5:14, 16

It's my firm contention that active Christians have opportunities to serve that even the angels don't have.

(Virgil Reed)

Certainly this passion to be His light, to take His message of Good News into my world, came from His calling in my very soul.

(Naomi Reed Rhode)

> **We are told to let our light shine, and if it does, we won't need to tell anybody it does. Lighthouses don't fire cannons to call attention to their shining—they just shine.**
>
> *Dwight L. Moody*

These words, "Let your lights so shine before men," were given to laymen and women. There's a great need today for active Christian laymen, so let's begin by defining the terms:

- A layman is one of the people;
- A Christian is one who is Christlike;
- An active person is one who gets things done.

So by combining these definitions, we can say that: "an active Christian layman is one of the people who is Christlike and actually gets things done." If you qualify for that definition, this message is addressed particularly to you. If you don't qualify for that definition, then this message is all the more for you.

Active Christian laymen and women are needed and needed badly today, for they can put in their words for Christ where preachers cannot and do not go. It's my firm contention that active Christians have opportunities to serve that even the angels don't have.

Not long ago, I heard a man make a very startling statement about a friend who had died. He said, "I lived and worked with John for ten years, and didn't know he was a Christian until I heard it announced at his funeral."

How do you act when you're working or relaxing with your fellow men and women? What kind of stories do you tell? What kind do you laugh at? What's your influence on your friends and family? As someone once said, "What you are thunders so loudly I cannot hear what you say."

As a layperson, what does Christ mean to you? Here are some of the fields of labor that we serve in, and for each of these fields Christ is as follows:

Artist	Altogether lovely
Architect	Cornerstone
Astronomer	Sun of Righteousness
Baker	The living bread

81

Biologist	Life
Builder	Sure Foundation
Carpenter	The door
Educator	The great teacher
Farmer	The sower and Lord of the harvest
Florist	Rose of Sharon, Lily of the Valley
Geologist	Rock of Ages
Horticulturist	True vine
Jeweler	Pearl of great price
Judge	Righteous Judge
Juror	Faithful and true witness
Lawyer	Counselor and advocate
Philanthropist	Unspeakable gift
Philosopher	Wisdom of God
Rancher	Good shepherd
Reporter	Good tidings
Sculptor	Living stone
Theologian	Author and finisher of our faith

As a layperson, what do you do to show forth your zeal for Christ and His Kingdom? Remember that the moon in all its beauty shines with only reflected light. Do we as Christians reflect the light of Christ?

(Excerpted from a message by Virgil Reed, date and place unknown.)

Naomi Responds

Let us lift high the cross in the market place, not leaving it on a hill between two thieves.

George McLeod

Flying home from a speaking engagement many years ago, I felt the heavy question on my soul: "Was I truly a light in a dark world? Would I ever have the privilege of seeing seed that's been planted and watered come to bear the fruit, spiritually, of new life in Christ?"

I shared this concern, this 'calling' with my husband Jim, and we prayed for God's harvest to be evident through my life, my speaking/writing, my relationships and our family. This, I believe, was a major revelation for me on the importance of being His messenger, His shining Light in a dark and needy world.

Elton Trueblood, the great theologian, said it so wonderfully, "The word laity does not appear in the Bible. Everyone is called into ministry; the task of spreading the Word of God and the responsibility for meeting the needs of a hurting world were never meant to be the assignments of an elite group of ordained church leaders. These 'callings' belong to all Christians."

Certainly this passion to be His light, to take His message of Good News into my world, came from His calling in my very soul.

Certainly also, it came from the incredible, consistent, passionate example of my parents. They chose to live His message, to speak His good news, and to share the hope that is only His to bring—to their family, their professions, and their relationships.

My niece's 4-year-old daughter came home from her Christian pre-school one day and announced with consternation: "Jesus wasn't in school today!" Puzzled, my niece, Kary, asked Kirsten's teacher what she meant. The teacher smiled, and said, "Oh, I know! Pastor John usually comes in every day, just before noon, to love the kids. He had an early lunch, and couldn't come yesterday." Thus, "Jesus wasn't in school" for that sweet little girl. She saw Jesus' life lived out in this pastor. How awesome!

God called Moses to be His spokesperson, to lead the people out of bondage in Egypt to the Promised Land. Wow, what an assignment that was! What a privilege! How shocking to hear Moses argue against this incredible honor, claiming the inability to speak!

God's answer was profound: "Who gave man his mouth?...Is it not I, the Lord? Now go; I will help you to speak and will teach you what to say" (Exodus 4:11). How much clearer, or reassuring, or empowering could it be?

Jesus Himself told His disciples: "For it will not be you speaking, but the Spirit of your Father speaking through you" (Matthew 10:20).

Whether artist, architect, astronomer, baker, biologist, builder, carpenter, dentist, educator, entrepreneur, farmer, florist, geologist, horticulturist, jeweler, judge, juror, lawyer, philanthropist, philosopher, physician, rancher, reporter, sculptor, professional speaker, theologian or writer, we have both a mandate and a great privilege: to share with passion and purpose His love and message with a broken world, and the power of His Spirit, our guide and accomplisher, to live the message of His grace with honor daily—the reflection of His light shining from our lives.

Chapter
12
Proud Rider Unhorsed

"Meanwhile Saul was still breathing out murderous threats against the Lord's disciples. He went to the high priest and asked him for letters to the synagogues in Damascus, so that if he found any there who belonged to the Way, whether men or women, he might take them as prisoners to Jerusalem. As he neared Damascus on his journey, suddenly a light from heaven flashed around him. He fell to the ground and heard a voice say to him, 'Saul, Saul, why do you persecute me?' 'Who are you, Lord?' Saul asked. 'I am Jesus, whom you are persecuting.'"

Acts 9:1-5

We believe in no weak gospel. It is a glorious gospel, an omnipotent gospel, the very power of God and the wisdom of God unto salvation.

(Virgil Reed)

Does my pride keep me on the 'horse' of my own abilities, will power, purpose and mission? Or do I hear His call and see the "light from heaven" flash?

(Naomi Reed Rhode)

> **For pride is spiritual cancer: it eats up the very possibility of love, or contentment, or even common sense.**
>
> *C.S. Lewis*

As he rides toward Jerusalem, there is evil intent in Saul's eyes. "These Christians must be captured and silenced, and that religion of the cross must be annihilated," he's thinking. Suddenly, he's thrown from his horse. A new sun is kindled in the heavens, putting out the glare of the ordinary sun. Dust-covered and bruised, Saul, blinded by the light, attempts to rise, calling out, "Who are you, Lord?"

Jesus answered: "I am the one you have been chasing. He who whips and scourges these Christians in Damascus whips and scourges me. It is not their backs that are bleeding, but my back. It is not their hearts that are breaking, it is my heart."

From this wild scene rises one destined to become the greatest preacher in all the ages—Paul, at whose command prison doors flew open, before whom soldiers turned pale, in whose hands a sea captain put control of his shipwrecked vessel, and whose epistles would proclaim the Resurrection.

We learn from this story that a spiritual uplifting is often preceded by a worldly fall. Proud and angry Saul, with all his fine education, tumbled in the dust. From that humiliating fall would arise Paul, the Apostle.

You'll never amount to much for God until you're brought low in some manner. You must go down before you go up. Joseph found the path to the Egyptian court through the pit into which his brothers threw him. Daniel would never have walked amidst the bronzed statues of lions that adorned the Babylonian throne if he had not first walked amidst real lions in the cave.

Those who graduate from the school of Christ with the highest honors have on their diplomas the seal of the lion's paw, the angry wave, the drop of a tear, or the brown scorch of persecuting fire. In nearly every case, there is no moral or spiritual elevation until there has been a thorough worldly upsetting.

We also learn from this story that the religion of Jesus Christ is not a small or cowardly one. Today, many say that it is only for men of small caliber, for women who have no capacity for reasoning, and for little children.

But look at the man in this text. Do you think that a religion that captured such a man as Paul is weak and powerless? He was a logician, a metaphysician, an all-conquering orator. He had a nature that could swamp the leading men of his day; when facing the Sanhedrin, he made them tremble. A master of Greek and Hebrew, he astonished the Cretans, the Corinthians and the Athenians by quoting from their own authors.

A religion that can capture a man like that has power in it. Where Paul leads, we can confidently follow. When a skeptic stands before you, take your New Testament and show him the picture of the intellectual giant of all ages, lying prostrate on the road to Damascus while his horse ran wildly away. Filled with hate and spite, and breathing out slaughter, he was determined to have the Christians captured and butchered. Can such a man ever become a Christian? Yes! And again, Yes!

We believe in no weak gospel. It is a glorious gospel, an omnipotent gospel, the very power of God and the wisdom of God unto salvation. Today, God can still overcome the persecutors who exist in various forms, some in our own homes and communities.

Just as Saul encountered Christ along the way to Damascus, may we today willingly say, "What will you have me do, Lord?" when we meet Him on the way.

(Excerpted from a message by Virgil Reed in Hawley, Minnesota, August 27, 1944)

Naomi Responds

**Pride is to the character what the attic is to the house—
the highest part, and generally the most empty.**

Henrietta C. Mears

As I read the title of my father's message, I felt the word "proud" resound in my spirit, and in my life. How about you? How easy it is for us to feel good about what we've done, been, accomplished, produced. We're taught that it's by our own plans, hands, will, and excellence that our world is created. How totally that denies the gifts we've been given by God: the gifts of time, health, incentive, creativity, compassion, and the compass to accomplish worthy work, rather than live a worthless and wasted life.

Saul was a proud man. By the standards of his day, he had every right to be proud. He was a trained Pharisee, had memorized the Torah (the first five Old Testament books). He knew the prophecies of Isaiah. He knew a Messiah would come to save His people. He knew what that Messiah would do, be, and accomplish.

And yet he failed to recognize and acknowledge that Jesus was indeed who He claimed to be—the Son of God.

Saul's fury was unleashed against the early followers of Jesus. He persecuted them; he ravaged their lives with his venom and hatred.

And, then it happened! A light from heaven flashed around him! He was thrown from the lofty height of horse and personal pride. He heard the voice of the Father calling him. Calling HIM! What a miracle of revelation, and life change. Only when God revealed Himself and His Son to Saul, did he believe, follow, and radically change.

The new man was Paul, certainly the most effective preacher, missionary to ever live. He had a new mission, a new message of hope, life, love, salvation, and peace for a hurting world.

What a powerful story! Certainly it gives me pause. How about you? Does my pride keep me on the 'horse' of my own abilities, will power, purpose and mission? Or do I hear His call and see the "light from heaven" flash? Do I fall to the ground in humble, oh, so humble desire, to follow Jesus into a dark and hurting world?

I saw that change lived in my father, Virgil Reed. I long to know that my children and grandchildren see that change in me, and will model it for generations to come.

Jesus promises "such a ride"—all the way to eternity. Come and ride with Him!

Omer and Naomi in Virgil's Reclaimed 'Coal Bin' Scout Den. (Relics, Crafts and a few Treasures from Theodore Roosevelt's Collection.)

'My Fathers Hands'
Securely Wrap My
Life With Love.

Naomi

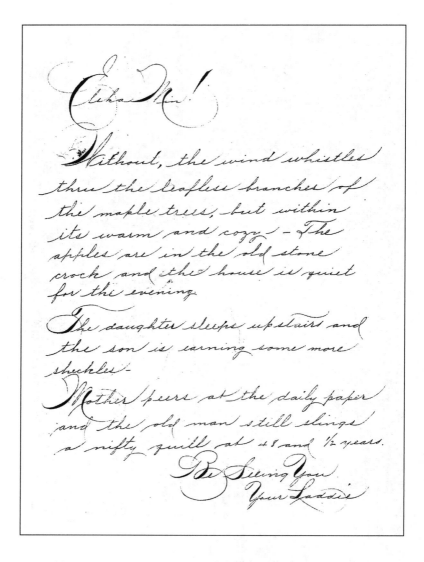

Elska Min!

Without, the wind whistles thru the leafless branches of the maple trees, but within its warm and cozy – The apples are in the old stone crock and the house is quiet for the evening.

The daughter sleeps upstairs and the son is earning some more sheckles –

Mother peers at the daily paper and the old man still slings a nifty quill at 48 and ½ years.

Be Seeing You.
Your Laddie

Beautiful love note from Virgil to Ellen on a cold winter night.

(My mother was Icelandic. "Elska Min' means "My Dear Ellen" in Icelandic.)

The Reed Family
Wilderness Boy Scout Camp
Park Rapids, Minnesota

Mess Hall Desert Time: Virgil (Camp Director), Ellen (Camp
Cook), Naomi ("Helper"), Omer (Boy Scout Camper)

The crown of home is Godliness.

The beauty of home is Order.

The blessing of home is Contentment.

The glory of home is Hospitality.

Virgil's Hand Calligraphed Favorite Credo on 'The Family'

Reed Family Crest

Teepee ~~~ Love of the outdoors
Bow & Arrow ~~~ Love of hunting, fishing, camping
Four reeds ~~~ Reed family members
Footprints ~~~ We are home ~~ You are always welcome
Smoke rising ~~~ Coffee pot is 'on'
Curved arrow ~~~ Indian sign language for Holy Spirit

Pictured Left:
The Virgil Reed
Family Logo and
Interpretation

Pictured Below:
In Tribute to Virgil A.
Reed (George Miller,
Chief Scout Executive
Phoenix, Arizona

IN TRIBUTE
to

VIRGIL A. REED
1901-1952

District Scout Executive
Roosevelt Council, Boy Scouts of America

A 'great man' was Virgil Reed, because he was what he was.

Although he was with us but a short time, his influence was felt throughout the council. A fine craftsman, an excellent counselor, a good woodsman, top scouter, a wonderful father and husband.

To his family, our love an appreciation for their courage and high example of faith and devotion.

Virgil Reed will live on in the memory of countless youth and adults alike. His influence on youth was wholesome, inspiring and with deep spiritual strength. No man better lived the tenets of the Scout Oath and Law.

The world is a better place in which to live because he was here.

May the great spirit of all Scouts be with us 'till we meet again".

Written in honor of Virgil – George Miller, Chief Scout Executive in Phoenix, Arizona

Chapter
13

Growing a Soul

"Consider how the lilies grow. They do not labor or spin. Yet I tell you, not even Solomon in all his splendor was dressed like one of these."

Luke 12:27

Like the great oak tree which braves the storm because its roots are deep and firm, the soul that's deeply rooted keeps growing in spite of trouble and temptation.

(Virgil Reed)

God's Word, the Bible, clearly outlines the best 'soul diet' to ensure that our lives will amaze people as they spring up out of seemingly barren ground, with His water, and His Sonshine, to delight and enrich the lives of others.

(Naomi Reed Rhode)

**Since the soul is large enough to contain the infinite
God, nothing less than Himself can satisfy or fill it.**

Edward B. Pusey

We love growth: the first blade of grass, the bud, the leaf, the pasture, the wheat, the cattle putting on weight, the family. A lack of growth usually signals something is wrong.

Growth is from God and is His way of reminding us that He is alive. We must reckon with it in all of life. The wisest physician can prescribe for the care of the body, but the growth of that body is God's secret.

A pastor may suggest ways that promote soul growth, but cannot make a soul grow. "Consider how the lilies grow." Soul growth is in God's hands. God's presence in a soul means there is life there, and life can never stand still. As it grows, the soul, like the body of a child, can experience growing pains, pains of doubt, discouragement and despair, but it still keeps on growing.

But, though the soul grows, it should never grow old. The body grows old and weak, but the soul need not. A God-filled soul grows more beautiful with age, and sweeter as the years go by.

As young people are taken through a period of Christian nurture and training, there's a risk that as they become full-fledged church members, they may think they're now safe and can rest. Then the soul ceases to grow and begins to dry up. God grieves when souls get clogged up and stop flowing and growing. The only way a soul can become fit for companionship with God is through constant growth.

How big is your soul right now? How much has it grown? How can we measure its growth? The same way we can measure the growth of a boy—by noting what he has outgrown: last year's clothes, his tricycle, the hobbyhorse.

Has your soul outgrown anything in the past year? Has it outgrown bigotry, pessimism, pride, jealousy, childish ideas of God? Is it firmly rooted in love and faith and hope? Like the great oak tree which braves the storm because its roots are deep and firm, the soul that's deeply rooted keeps growing in spite of trouble and temptation.

Carrying a Bible around is no evidence of soul growth. It may enhance our reputation, which is what others think of us, but is no indication of our character, which is what we really are. A beautiful character produces a beautiful life in which dwells a beautiful and growing soul.

Has your soul grown? Is it still growing? Can you test its growth by a beautiful life that is serving the Master? Lord, grant that we may grow in grace.

(Excerpted from a message by Virgil Reed, date and place unknown.)

Naomi Responds

The body—that is but dust; the soul is a bud of eternity.

Nathaniel Culverwell

Have you been to Arizona in the Springtime? It's amazing to drive through the desert, the mountains, the red rocks of Sedona, and see the incredible carpet of profuse and 'hilarious' African Daisies. Yellow, orange, white, gold, crimson!

I remember asking naively when we first moved to Arizona, "Who planted all those incredible flowers?" With knowing smiles, the answer was, "No one. They just come up and bloom every spring."

What a great picture of the Luke passage, and Jesus' answer: *"Consider how the lilies grow. They do not labor or spin."* Indeed, God has planted the seeds of the African Daisies in the dry, parched ground.

With the right amount of water and sunshine (or is it 'Sonshine'?) and at the very right time, they peek through the ground and blossom into a glorious affirmation of God's beautiful surprises to weary and beauty-starved travelers.

And, what a dynamic picture of 'soul growth' for each of us, as followers of Jesus. He plants the seed of belief in *our* dry parched ground. It's watered by the Word of God, by His followers, and by prayer. And then it blooms outrageously for the beauty of a hurting world.

Isn't it interesting that often we see soul growth in people as the physical body is diminishing? How often have you sat at the bedside of a very ill person, or even a dying person, and seen the glorious health and beauty of their souls, even as their body was dying?

My mother, Ellen Goodman Reed, was such a witness to God's work in her life. She had miraculously survived one of the very first, experimental open-heart surgeries when I was just a sophomore in high school. She lived 10 years after that surgery, wonderful years, to see me through college, marriage and my first two children.

At age 24, I sat on her hospital bed in Two Harbors, Minnesota, day after day. It was bitter cold, 24 degrees below zero outside, and so cold in my heart. My mother was dying. Correction! My mother's body was dying. Her soul, which had grown for years, deep into the soil of God's love and grace, was bursting forth in the bloom of promised life eternal.

On that Tuesday morning, she proclaimed to me that she was going to die that day. I hurried to ask her physician if he thought she was about to die. He denied that probability, and said she seemed to be better, in fact.

Moments later, Mother said, "Naomi, there are several things I want to tell you before I die." She proceeded to instruct me with wisdom only a mother can give, told me what a dear and good daughter I had been, and then paused. Looking toward the heavens, as if she saw them open, she said, "The Lord be praised. The Lord be praised." And then—she died!

Or did she? Did her soul indeed blossom into full growth, a thing of incredible beauty, to be remembered forever and ever? Her body died, but her soul rocketed into eternity to join the saints of all time and the Heavenly Father she loved so dearly.

It seems everywhere we turn today, we read about or hear about the best diets for our bodies. But God's Word, the Bible, clearly outlines the best 'soul diet' to ensure that our lives will amaze people as they spring up out of seemingly barren ground, with His water, and His Sonshine, to delight and enrich the lives of others.

So may it be—for me—and for you!

Chapter

14

Going to the Father

"I go to my Father."
John 14:12

Some call God the King Eternal; some call him infinite Jehovah. But we, as His children, are privileged to call Him simply Our Father. To live daily in this simplicity is to live like Christ.

(Virgil Reed)

We are God's children! What an awesome concept. As a Father, He loves, guides, cares, chastens, corrects, holds, forgives, and encompasses.

(Naomi Reed Rhode)

Our destination is home with our Father in heaven. It is so easy on this journey to lose sight of our destination and to focus on the detours of this life instead. This life is only the trip to get home.

Dr. Bob Snyder

You can unlock a man's whole life if you watch the words he uses most. We each have words which, though we're unaware of it, we always work with, and which really express all we mean by life, or have found out of it.

Did you ever notice Christ's favorite words? If you have, you must have been struck by two things, their simplicity and their fewness. Some half-dozen expand on His theology, and without exception, these words are humble, elementary, simple words—such words as World, Life, Trust and Love.

When He came, there was no word rich enough to carry the new truth He was bringing to men; and so He imported into religion one of the grandest words in the human language. He transfigured it, and he gave it back to the world illuminated and transformed. That word was Father.

Surely it's the most touching sight of the world's past to see God's only begotten Son coming down from heaven to try to teach the stammering inhabitants of this poor planet to say, "Our Father."

Some call God the King Eternal; some call him infinite Jehovah. But we, as His children, are privileged to call Him simply Our Father. To live daily in this simplicity is to live like Christ.

To live like Christ is not to agonize daily over details, to make anxious comparisons with what we do and what He did; it's a much simpler thing—it's to re-echo Christ's words, "Our Father." It's to have that calm, patient, assured spirit, which reduces life simply to this—a going to the Father.

The one thing which steadied and ordered the life of Jesus Christ was His awareness that He was "going home to His Father." The one thing that gave unity to Christ's life, and harmony and success, was that during His whole life He never forgot the word "Father" for one moment.

In the first memorable sentence when he spoke to his mother in the presence of the doctors in the temple, He used that word, "Did you not know that I must be about my Father's business?" And for the rest of His life on earth, the great name was always hovering on his lips or bursting from His heart. His first words in the ministry—"about my Father's business," and among his last words—"I go to my Father."

Few men, I suppose, feel life doesn't need explaining. Even the wisest mind can't understand all of life. What is life? Where am I going? Where do I come from? The poet answers that life is a sleep, a dream, a shadow, a vapor that appears for a little while, and then vanishes, like bubbles which form and then burst upon the river of time. That explains nothing. It's taking refuge in mystery. "Where am I going?" The poet answers, "I'm going to the unknown."

What's the atheist's answer to what is life? It's just the opposite. He knows no unknown; he understands all. There's nothing more than we can see or feel. "Where am I going?" The atheist says, "I go to dust." He says further, "Death ends all." And this explains nothing. It's worse than mystery—it's contradiction; it's utter darkness.

But the Christian's answer explains something. Where is he going? "I go to my Father." This isn't a definition of his death—there is no death in Christianity—it's the definition of the Christian life. All the time, the Christian is "going to the Father."

Some travel swiftly; some are long upon the road. Some meet many pleasant adventures by the way; others pass through fire and peril. But though the path be straight or winding, and though the pace be quick or slow, it is "going to the Father."

Therefore, let us be patient, for we haven't yet arrived; we've only set out upon the way. Let's remember that we're going to the Father. O let us live like it, more simple, uncomplaining, useful, separate, joyful as those who march to music, yet sober as those who are following Christ. The road is long, high road and low road; but we shall soon be home. We're going to the Father.

(Excerpted from a message by Virgil Reed, date and place unknown.)

Naomi Responds

Be still, and in the quiet moments, listen to the voice of your heavenly Father. His words can renew your spirit. No one knows you and your needs like He does.

Janet Weaver

I love the way my Dad started this sermon, talking about the power of words! As a professional speaker, I'm in awe of words, their meaning, their significance, their life-changing power.

In the Old Testament book of Amos, the prophet is warning the people that God would indeed punish their disobedience, their turning from His 'words.' He says there will not only be an exile and famine of food, but there will be a "famine of words."

When I read this phrase and comprehended it the first time, I sat stunned! What would it be like to experience a "famine of words"? God would be silent. Not speaking through the prophets, the Holy Scriptures, audibly, or in one's heart—just silence.

This actually happened! For four hundred years, between the end of the Old Testament and the beginning of the New Testament, God was silent.

My curiosity was further piqued. What broke the "famine of words"? In essence, it was an angel appearing to a young woman, Mary, declaring that the Messiah, the Promised One, would be conceived in her womb and, as a virgin, would give birth to the Son of God.

Another "word" for Messiah, Jesus, was "The Word." In the opening chapter of the Gospel of John, we read: "The Word became flesh and dwelt among us" (John 1:14). Incredible! The Word came, breaking the famine of words, to live, die, rise from the dead, ascend to heaven, to come back indwelling us as believers, so we would always have 'The Word' dwelling in our hearts.

This Word provides us always with the words we need to speak to a hurting and needy world. Plus, we have The Word of God, the Holy Scriptures. How wealthy we are with His words to read, to meditate on, and to be interpreted by The Word within us.

And then: the real point of Dad's message! When The Word came (Jesus), He introduced a new word to us—the word, Father! God as

Creator, Sustainer, Alpha, Omega, Messiah, The Holy One of Israel, now becomes Abba Father to me—and to you.

We are God's *children*! What an awesome concept. As a Father, He loves, guides, cares, chastens, corrects, holds, forgives, and encompasses. In life and in death I have access to the Father. The door is always open. I can always go to my Father.

In November 2003, my mother-in-law, 94-year-old Agnes Mesenburg, went home to be with the Lord. Born in Norway of Swedish parents, she had come to America as a child, and lived with us for many years prior to her death. In her autobiography, published in 2001, she wrote about her favorite Swedish hymn which, in English, is titled "Children of the Heavenly Father."

She had asked that it be played at her funeral. At the memorial service in Phoenix, prior to her burial in Minnesota, six of her great grandchildren played it on violins, cello and harp, while their teacher sang a verse in Swedish. The words of that wonderful old hymn express it well: "Children of the Heavenly Father, Safely in His bosom gather...Neither life nor death shall ever, From the Lord His children sever..."

What a wonderfully reassuring thought: that as children of Our Heavenly Father, we can always depend on His presence and protection—in this life, and forever in the next.

Chapter
15
The Stewardship of Time

"Therefore keep watch because you do not know when the owner of the house will come back—whether in the evening, or at midnight, or when the rooster crows, or at dawn."

Mark 13:35

Time is fleeting, and writes its message on our hair and faces and forms, and on our dispositions and our character.

(Virgil Reed)

How many years will He give me? How many years will He give you? Maybe just months, or even days, but surely, surely, He wants us to meet Him daily, to meet Him so our steps will be guided, our way made clear, and our lives blessed.

(Naomi Reed Rhode)

**Time is the deposit each one has in the bank of God,
and no one knows the balance.**

Ralph W. Sockman

Space and time are the twin mysteries which forever baffle the questing mind of man. Men peer into the skies through ever larger telescopes, as if to find an end to the distant fields of blue. Yet the work of the Creator always exceeds the effort to put a fence at the end of space.

Eternity is too small a word to express the beginning back yonder of time, and its endlessness in ages yet unborn. Time baffles man by its distance both backward and forward from the hour in which he stands.

Jesus recognized the problem. His words, "Therefore keep watch," challenge his hearers to an awareness of the mystery of time. Life at best is uncertain, and time must be considered as a loan made by God to His children. No one knows when that loan will be recalled. At any hour, we may be called to give an account of our stewardship.

"Therefore keep watch," said the Master to His disciples, but it was spoken to every human being in every age. Time is fleeting, and writes its message on our hair and faces and forms, and on our dispositions and our character.

We try hard to ward off the telltale signs of oncoming age, grabbing at every fad or fancy which promises to restore the lost radiance of youth, while beauty shop operators profit by our attempts to conquer time.

Centuries before Christ, an Egyptian pharaoh announced that he had conquered time by having constructed an enormous statue, which came to be called "The Sphinx." He boasted that he had made it so solid and so huge that even eternity could not destroy it.

Today, the sands drift endlessly about it and the once proud face is broken and marred by the centuries of change. It has become a lasting reminder of the futility of human effort when pitted against the power of time.

Christian stewardship recognizes time as sacred. It views all of life as a loan made by God to His children. Because time is so important a factor in life, the faithful Christian will desire to keep close to

God and will use well every moment of that part of eternity allotted to him. Not a week should pass without at least an hour being set aside to meet with Christ's followers for worship and prayer.

Nor should the worship of God be limited to public services. The faithful Christian steward will gladly spend a portion of every day in prayer and meditation. Each morning will bring a new recognition of God's goodness, each day a new oath of allegiance to Him.

A good steward of God's time will endeavor to keep close to the heart of his Creator, and to be busy about matters of great importance. Life is too short to be wasted in futile and meaningless effort.

Every pastor is frequently asked about which recreational activities and habits are right and wrong for the Christian. But, for the average Christian, the question is not whether a recreation or practice is right or wrong, but what important matters will be left undone while God's time is used for play? Life is too short to be lived on the level of petty uselessness when the door to God's high purpose has swung wide open.

We don't know when the stewardship of our time will be called into account: perhaps in the evening, or at midnight, or at dawn. As the Master holds open the gate to eternity, perhaps a smile will cross His face when he sees us, and speaks words that will set the heavenly joy-bells ringing: "Welcome, good and faithful servant, enter into the joy of the Lord."

(Excerpted from a message by Virgil Reed, date and time unknown.)

Naomi Responds

Be wise in the use of time. The question of life is not, "How much time have we?" The question is, "What shall we do with it?"

Anna Robertson Brown

As the sun was setting, reflected with blazing glory in the waters of Bad Axe Lake in Northern Minnesota's Wilderness Boy Scout Camp, a family of four would find their way silently through the woods to a private camp site. Four simple logs, laid in a square, surrounded a small campfire, warming our hearts and focusing our souls inward, upward, and outward to each other.

Each evening after my mother as Camp Cook finished the evening meal, and Dad as Camp Director finished his duties, we would meet. I was a young girl those many summers, and my brother Omer was a young teenager.

Why the ceremony? Why the focus of our hearts?

Family time, yes—away from the busyness of running a camping program. Quiet time, yes—a retreat from the challenges, and exhaustion of hard physical and emotional work.

But, there was more, so much more—time set aside for our "Reed Family Altar." Our time to say to the Lord, "Thank you. Thank you for a world of woods, winds, waves, wilderness. Thank you for a world of work, words, woodcrafting and wild adventure. But thank you mostly for Omnipotence, Omniscience, Omnipresence, for Sovereign plans, grace, atonement, and sacrifice. Thank you for the mystery of life and the promise of eternity."

Time! As I reread my father's words about "The Stewardship of Time," I thought of those times, allocated for the richness of togetherness, worship, and contemplation. There were evenings we worshiped together, laughed together, read Scripture together, told stories, and I'm sure there were evenings when tears were shed, disappointments shared, differences aired, and even silence celebrated. But it was important!

None of us knows how many days/years of life we have. But we all know the choices of how we 'steward' that time. We are indeed the sum total of all our choices, all our time spent. And, one day, we will indeed "give an account" of how we spent our special allotment of time.

It's intriguing to note that God gives some the gift of just minutes, and some the gift of decades: six, eight, ten. And then this "mystery gift" is over. The breath leaves our bodies, and our souls enter the eternity that was paid for by either Christ's sacrifice, or our own choice to deny Him.

Many years have passed. I've lived in the clatter of city life, the hustle of busyness, the decades of raising children, packing lunches, helping with homework, speaking at seminars and conventions, marrying, burying, befriending, traveling, exploring, writing, reading, caring, loving, planning.

Much has changed over those years, but the one thing that hasn't changed is the Word of God. He is immutable, unchangeable, the eternal, all-wise God. And, for me, it's still important to meet Him in Spirit, in truth, and in His Word, every day.

No longer do I walk through the woods to a campfire setting. Instead I meet Him on my "prayer and praise patio" in Phoenix, Arizona, where we live. Almost every morning I'm there. He is there. In the winter, I light a fire in the fireplace on the patio, snuggle up in my afghan, light a candle, and warm my hands with a cup of hot coffee.

In the hot summer months, early/early mornings are cool, and with the overhead fan the patio is beautiful. The birds meet me there, the fountain splashes musically, and I say "hello" to my best friend, and prepare for the day.

And when we travel, which is much of the year, I take this "patio" with me, reconstructing it in hotel rooms, hallways, balconies, beach side, and even small bathrooms to protect waking a sleeping spouse.

It's my place, my place to meet with Him. It's a choice, not a legalistic mandate; a privilege, not a "should do." It's a time saver, not a time waster!

How many years will He give me? How many years will He give you? Maybe just months, or even days, but surely, surely, He wants us to meet Him daily, to meet Him so our steps will be guided, our way made clear, and our lives blessed with the power of His message, His legacy, and His will in our work, our mission, our play.

Thank you, Father, for parents who knew the importance of time. Though they both died young, I have no doubt their eternal legacy was far beyond the average life on this earth. And I'm blessed to have been, and to be for eternity, their daughter, the one who learned from the legacy of Virgil and Ellen Reed.

Chapter
16

The Stewardship
of Grace

"Minister...one to another, as good stewards of the manifold grace of God."

1 Peter 4:10, KJV

A true steward of the manifold gift of God, in giving and laboring for others, is paving his own highway to the place you and I expect to attain.

(Virgil Reed)

Grace, amazing grace—how sweet the sound! It's a word that's whispered, sung, shared, applied, understood, believed, and unfathomable!

(Naomi Reed Rhode)

As the grace of God changes a man's heart, this is the great evidence of the change; that he begins to grow in love, to lay aside self-seeking, and to live for others.

Francis Paget

Had Peter challenged his readers to be good stewards of the money they earned, that would have tested their loyalty. Had he called upon them to be good stewards of their leisure hours, that would have thrust a challenge into their busy lives.

But to tell them to be good stewards of the "manifold grace of God," that took them into a realm of uncertainty and mystery. The word "manifold" means many diverse elements. For example, in an automobile engine, it refers to many ports or openings.

"The grace of God" is one of the most frequently used phrases in the New Testament and many worship services end with this benediction: "The grace of the Lord Jesus Christ be with you." It is one of the most beautiful and meaningful phrases in all the history of religious experience. But what exactly does it mean?

Among the many suggested definitions of the term, one stands out above the others. The grace of God is the love of God poured upon man, not according to his worthiness, but according to his need. It is bigger than love, bigger than sacrifice; it is as big as life itself. God sent Christ, not because men were worthy of Him, but because they were in great need. That is the grace of God.

Most of us realize that God has abundantly blessed us in manifold ways. It should be noted, however, that the proclamation of the fact that we have received the benefits of the grace of God is only one part of our text. There is another part that is no less significant and even more challenging. It tells us that the grace of God was not given to us as God's children for us to boast about, but for us to be "good stewards" of His gifts.

When we give ourselves to God's cause and work, we are building a mansion on our lot in Heaven. A true steward of the manifold gift of God, in giving and laboring for others, is paving his own highway to the place you and I expect to attain.

I recently saw a copy of a letter sent to a radio preacher by one of his listeners, after the preacher announced that we would be speaking on the following Sunday about Heaven.

"I am interested in that land," the listener wrote, "because I have held a clear title to a bit of property there for over 55 years. I did not buy it. It was given to me without price. But the donor purchased it for me at tremendous sacrifice...It is not a vacant lot. For more than half a century, I have been sending materials, out of which the greatest architect of the universe has been building a home for me which will never need to be remodeled or repaired, because it will suit me perfectly, individually, and will never grow old. Termites can never undermine its foundations, for they rest upon the Rock of Ages. Fire cannot destroy it. Floods cannot wash it away...

"I cannot reach my home in that city of gold without passing through the dark valley of shadows. But I am not afraid, because the best friend I ever had went through the same valley long ago and drove away all its gloom."

The letter concludes: "I hope to hear your sermon on Heaven next Sunday, but I have no assurance that I shall be able to. My ticket for Heaven has no date marked for the journey, no return coupon, no permit for baggage. I shall meet you there some day."

Can we as stewards write such a letter? Can we know that our talents and our time have been well cared for by our stewardship? Are we true stewards of the manifold gifts of God?

(Excerpted from a message by Virgil Reed, date and place unknown.)

Naomi Responds

The love that gives, that loves the unlovely and the unlovable, is given a special name in the New Testament—grace.

Oswald C.J. Hoffmann

We are called, we are challenged, to be "good stewards of the manifold grace of God." The complexity of that calling is, in and of itself, a lifetime quest to discover, to realize, and to execute the full measure of the gifts God has bestowed on us through no deserving of our own, no merit, just His "manifold grace."

I immediately focus on the privilege of being a steward of the legacy of faith given to me by my father and mother, the education, freedom and opportunities I experience in our country, and the time, talent and possessions He has given me to responsibly share with others—all because of His manifold grace!

Grace, amazing grace—how sweet the sound! It's a word that's whispered, sung, shared, applied, understood, believed, and unfathomable! It's unmerited. It's extended with a loving heart and hand, completely redemptive for undeserving souls.

How the world tries to echo the effectiveness and power of grace. We extend "grace periods," we offer "grace" at mealtime, we address royalty as "Your Grace," we forgive because of grace, and we "grace" our friends and family with our presence and love. We do all this because we are in awe of the riches of His grace. And, we desire to "minister to one another as good stewards of the manifold grace of God."

One of the most indelible examples of grace in literature is found in the 19th century novel, *Les Misérables*, by Victor Hugo. The author tells the story of Jean Valjean, who has been released from jail after serving years for stealing bread. He seeks lodging at a Monastery, and in spite of the hospitality of the bishop, he steals the silverware to use to purchase food and lodging.

Constables quickly arrest Valjean, and return him to the monastery to face his despicable act, and his certain accuser. The bishop immediately realizes what has occurred. Instead of accusing

Valjean, he reaches for the silver candlesticks, hands them to him and says to the constables, "I gave him the silver." Then he says to Valjean, "Here are the candlesticks I gave you also. You forgot to take them with you."

Valjean's unforgettable words of response are, "This day my life has been unalterably changed by grace." The rest of the story is the incredible "living out of grace," through every act and life Valjean intersects and influences.

What an awesome example of grace! What a mandate for stewardship! We have been blessed with the "manifold grace of God." How then shall we live, but to share this grace, to extend this compassion and love, and to touch and change a hurting world with His love?

"Minister…one to another…as good stewards of the manifold grace of God."

Chapter
17
The Power of Pentecost

"He commanded them that they should not depart from Jerusalem, but wait for the promise of the Father..."

Acts 1:4

What a tragedy it is that so many Christians are content to claim their share in what was done at Calvary, but never go on and claim their portion in the gift of Pentecost!

(Virgil Reed)

The power of the Holy Spirit is meant to flow freely through my life as a flood of water, to nourish the hearts of those I encounter.

(Naomi Reed Rhode)

> Power depends on good connections. The train with the locomotive, machinery with the engine; the electrical mechanism with the powerhouse. And in the Christian life the follower of Jesus with the Spirit of Jesus.
>
> *S.D. Gordon*

Jesus seldom commanded His followers to tarry or wait. His commands were "to go and tell," "go and teach," "go and baptize," "go and win." But he charged them here to wait, to tarry until they would be filled with power from on high.

Power! How we all crave and long for power! The power of wealth is wonderful. It is the genie of Aladdin's lamp. Men command it, and things are done. The power of knowledge is marvelous. Men who know, and know how to use their knowledge, have power.

The Day of Pentecost was the day when the church was clothed in power. Some think of it as our spiritual "Fourth of July," when the church was constituted. We must all agree it was the day when the church was baptized with power. The Day of Pentecost will never be repeated. There is no more need of its being repeated than that of the Crucifixion and Resurrection.

What a tragedy that so many Christians are content to claim their share in what was done at Calvary, but never go on and claim their portion in the gift of Pentecost!

When Peter preached to the household of Cornelius, the Holy Spirit fell on all those who heard the word, and he commanded them to be baptized (in water) in the name of the Lord. There was both water and Spirit baptism.

Those at Ephesus, who had received only John's baptism and had not heard of the coming of the Holy Spirit, were baptized in the name of the Lord Jesus. When Paul laid his hands upon them, the Holy Spirit came on them. They received both water and Spirit baptism.

If the church needed this Spirit power then, we sorely need it now. The form of the Spirit's coming is symbolic of His mighty power. He came at Pentecost "as the rushing of a mighty wind."

In nature, there are various forms of this rushing mighty wind. One is the cyclone, rotating with terrific speed about a calm center of low atmospheric pressure. Another is the hurricane, reaches a velocity of one hundred miles an hour or more. It has power to bend metal light posts as if they were made of straw.

A third mighty wind is the tornado, with its funnel-shaped cloud accompanied by violent eddies. The barometric pressure falls so rapidly that buildings are lifted from the ground and burst open by the air confined in them, like over-inflated toy balloons.

The church often through the centuries—too often—has spread its sails to catch the favor of man instead of the favor of God, becoming many times as still and immobile as the ship described in Coleridge's "Ancient Mariner."

You recall the story of how the sailors shot the albatross, killing the bird that caused the breezes to blow, and found themselves on a smooth, silent sea, without breeze or wind. In Coleridge's words, they then sat: "As idle as a painted ship, Upon a painted ocean."

When the church quenches the Holy Spirit, which causes the heavenly breezes to blow, it finds itself motionless and powerless, upon a windless, breathless, silent sea: "As idle as a painted ship, Upon a painted ocean."

No man is saner than when he is filled with the Holy Spirit. The Holy Spirit is not fanaticism, but sanity. The Holy Spirit descended on Jesus in the form of a dove, the emblem of purity. What a glorious privilege is ours! By the power of the Spirit, we may rise above the troubles and annoyances of this world.

The story is told of an aviator who soared in his plane and, as he soared, he saw a rat gnawing at some vital part of his machine. He couldn't turn loose the controls and get to the rat, but he knew if it continued to gnaw, the plane would be wrecked.

Then, he did the only thing he could, turning the nose of the plane up and climbing into the high thin atmosphere where oxygen is scarce. As he did, he watched the rat and, in the thin atmosphere, saw it grow weaker and cease gnawing. Soon the rat fell off and he was delivered from his trouble.

In the same way, by the indwelling of the Holy Spirit, we can rise above trials and annoyances and on unto the very door of heaven.

(Excerpted from a message by Virgil Reed, given on June 24, 1945.)

Naomi Responds

**Know where your strength comes from. It is only the
Holy Spirit who can make a message good and fruitful.**

Corrie ten Boom

As I read again my father's words about the power of
Pentecost, I'm awed by the radical change this power made
in the lives of His disciples and His followers.

It began with the chosen 12, the disciples. These followers of
Jesus through His earthly ministry walked with him, witnessed His
miracles, and experienced His powerful presence. And then, they fell
asleep while He anguished and prayed in the Garden of Gethsemane.
They deserted Him, denied Him, and even betrayed Him. We see
them as such wimps, such fickle followers, such shortsighted, undeserving, unfaithful men.

And then, the Crucifixion! The Resurrection! The risen Christ's
appearance to the disciples, the Ascension, and the promised "power
of Pentecost."

And everything changed! These disturbingly fickle, weak men literally changed the world with the power of the Gospel of Jesus
Christ. And eventually, they were all willing to give their lives, and
most actually were martyred for their faith.

What a radical change! What could have caused it? Their will
power? Their guilt? Their convictions? One thing is certainly clear:
it was not their own power. No, it was the power of the Holy Spirit
dwelling in and through them. It was the mighty wind of His glorious Spirit at Pentecost that blew through these weak disciples, and all
the followers of Jesus, both men and women. They started an unending spiritual revolution of faith, based solely on the grace of our Lord
Jesus Christ, and the power of His Spirit.

I remember the first time I heard Bruce Wilkinson, founder of
Walk Thru the Bible Ministries, speak. I sat mesmerized by the real-
ity of his teaching. Certainly I had known the theology of the Holy
Spirit before. But somehow, this time, Bruce made 'the power of
Pentecost' become crystal clear.

This filling of the Holy Spirit was for all believers! When we believe in God's Son, His Spirit comes in to us all, and fills us all with His power. It's free and fully ours, this power! No one has more of the Holy Spirit's power than another person. We all have it all!

Why, then, do we feel and experience overwhelming power in some believers' lives, and so little in others? Scripture is clear that our unconfessed sin is a choice to block this power of His Spirit, thus "grieving the Spirit" greatly!

Most of us have experienced the power of a great waterfall, rushing to provide its nourishing water to the fields, woods and crops below. Unencumbered, the power and beauty of this flow of water causes us to stand in silence and awe midst its thunder and power.

We've also seen how that same water can be dammed up, prevented from flowing freely, and rechanneled in totally different directions and for different purposes.

How like our lives that is. The power of the Holy Spirit is meant to flow freely through my life as a flood of water, to nourish the hearts of those I encounter. It's only my self-focus, greed and even disbelief that thwart His best and His highest for my life—for His life lived out through me.

Recently our daughter and son-in-law purchased some land in the rolling hills of Kentucky. Our 3-fi year old grandson, Broder, was telling me about the water on the property. "Amma, it's so beautiful. It's a fountain of water, lots and lots of it, and we call it a creek!"

When people see me—when they see you—do they see the fountain, the creek, the waterfall of His love? And, do they hear the wind of His Spirit, the Pentecostal Power, blowing freely, changing lives, unencumbered by the blockage of self and our own 'trying'? So may it be, for His Glory!

Chapter
18
The Place
Called Calvary

"When they were come to the place, which is called
Calvary, there they crucified him."

Luke 23:33

Here on the hill called "The Skull," the Son of God struggled with the destructive forces of hell, and died one of the most horrible forms of death—crucifixion!

(Virgil Reed)

We receive His grace, His forgiveness and His peace through this unfathomable sacrifice of the Holy Son of God.

(Naomi Reed Rhode)

The cross is God's connection between time and eternity. He planned it from before the foundation of the world, and it is intended for the whole world.

Richard C. Halverson

We have heard the word "Calvary" so often, and used it so much, and connected it so much with the greatest of all experiences, that we have lost its root meaning. Calvary is a hideous word and presents a horrible idea. It is the Latin word for "skull," and, in Aramaic, is called "Golgotha."

Here on the hill called "The Skull," the Son of God struggled with the destructive forces of hell, and died one of the most horrible forms of death—crucifixion! But even death could not keep Him in its shadows. "With a mighty triumph o'er His foes, He arose a victor from the dark domain, And He lives forever with His saints to reign."

Let us look more closely at what occurred on this hill called "The Skull." Calvary was a place of *guilt.* "And the malefactors, one on the right hand and the other on the left," were crucified with Jesus. They were evildoers, like Barabbas, who would have been one of them had Pilate not released him.

Calvary was a place of *compassion.* The greatest plea that ever came from the lips of man was that of Jesus when He cried, "Father, forgive them, for they know not what they do."

It was a place of base *irreverence.* "And parting his garments among them, they cast lots." At the foot of the cross of a crucified Savior, men were so debased that they gambled over His clothing.

It was a place of *derision.* "The rulers scoffed at him, the soldiers mocked him, and the multitude railed against him," even as the most sublime scene ever witnessed by human eyes was being enacted, and when tender love was offering itself for cruel sin.

It was a place of *testimony.* A superscription was placed over Him, reading, "This is Jesus of Nazareth, the King of the Jews." Pilate wrote it in a fit of stubborn rebellion and retaliation.

He never dreamed how significant it was to be. It was written in Greek, the language of culture, art and philosophy. All culture, to be real and abiding, must make Jesus its center. All true art must find its inspiration in Jesus, and all philosophy must begin and end with Him.

It was written in Latin, the language of authority, law and power, and in Hebrew, the language of divine revelation, spiritual wisdom and moral sanity. If man is to know God, he must know Him who hangs on the cross.

Calvary was a place of *prayer*. How significant is the simple prayer of the penitent thief in that dark hour when he cried, "Jesus, remember me when Thou comest into Thy kingdom." He became the morning star of hope for every lost man on earth. His faith reached out and took hold of the throne of mercy and, when he had prayed, he felt the loving and everlasting arms of God thrown about him as he was lifted out of sin into salvation.

Calvary thus became a place of *salvation*. Jesus, with His heart sensitive to every cry of a lost soul, heard the prayer of the penitent thief and, even in His agony, said, "Verily I say unto thee, today thou shalt be with me in paradise."

Calvary was a place of *miracle*. For six long, slow-moving, mystic hours during midday, darkness came upon the whole land. God's great wrath was revealed in shutting off the light of day and His great mercy was revealed in opening up the Holy of Holies. No longer must the sinner, poor and needy, approach God through human priesthood. Every soul seeking a Savior comes now directly into His presence and receives forgiveness for sin.

Calvary was a place of *victory through death*. "And having said this, he gave up the ghost." And it marked the most glorious dawn of a new day for the whole world of sin and shame when the fairest of ten thousand, the mighty Son of God, died so that men lost and undone, men burdened and depressed, men marred and wrecked, might be saved. Calvary was indeed the place of *victory through death*.

Finally, Calvary was a place of invitation. The gesture of the cross is the wide-open arms, saying, "Come unto me."

"Come from every nation and tribe, every kindred and tongue....Whoever will, let him take the water of life freely."

(Excerpted from a message by Virgil Reed, date unknown.)

Naomi Responds

There is something in Calvary that passes our
understanding, and the words about the Precious
Blood should never be read or sung except on the
knees of our spirit.

Amy Carmichael

It's Monday of Holy Week as I read again this powerful excerpt from my father's message about Calvary. He delivered it decades ago, about a time, a place, a horrific encounter with the forces of evil, and the prevailing victory of our Heavenly Father's plan—a plan for you and a plan for me. The words are so powerful. This place, Calvary, so painful.

Is it just a tragic story, a travesty on an innocent man? Or is it the pivotal turning point of all history, the pivotal point of personal decision for life eternal for each of us?

In the Spring of 2004, Mel Gibson's film, "The Passion of the Christ," was released. All the publicity, all the interviews, all the articles about it, could not adequately prepare one's soul for the force of the reality of that event at Calvary. The last hours of Christ's life were portrayed in detail far beyond our personal tolerance, and yet, far from the full truth of His persecution and suffering.

Certainly we'll never be the same as we sip the cup of communion, the remembrance of His blood shed for our sin. Surely we'll never be the same as we receive the broken bread, symbolic of His broken body. We receive His grace, His forgiveness and His peace through this unfathomable sacrifice of the Holy Son of God.

Studying the details of Calvary further expands our understanding of the omnipotence of the Father, of His Son, and His plan. The finger pointing of blame is dissolved in the words of Jesus Himself, as He proclaims to Pilate, "No man taketh my life. I have come to give my life." Profound, simple, direct!

This death was "according to the Scriptures" (1 Corinthians 15:3). In Isaiah 53, the prophet proclaimed that the coming Messiah would be "wounded for our transgressions," and would innocently be "an offering for our sin." Jesus himself proclaimed that He would be mocked, scourged and crucified (Matthew 20:19).

Detail after detail was prophesied, fulfilled, and new life offered through His sacrifice and forgiveness. All of it—accomplished at Calvary! Calvary, that place of "compassion, irreverence, derision, testimony, prayer, salvation, miracle, victory through death, and invitation."

Oswald Chambers once declared: "The cross was not something that happened to Jesus. He came to die; the Cross was His purpose in coming." As we read in Revelation 13:8, He is "the Lamb slain from the foundation of the world."

Calvary! Never has there been a place more profoundly suited for the phrase, "Come and See, Go and Tell." Tell the Good News. It is finished! The battle is won! Death could not hold Him! The tomb is empty! He is risen! He is Risen Indeed!

Chapter

19

The Presence

"Did not our hearts burn within us while he talked to us on the road, while he opened to us the scriptures?"

Luke 24:32

Today, whether men admit it or not, there is a yearning for the presence of Christ, for the guest at the cottage door of Emmaus. Christ is here with us today, as he was with those disciples on the road 2,000 years ago.

(Virgil Reed)

Christ's presence when we're weary, dejected, needing comfort, needing perspective in our hurting worlds, is not only promised, but is reality for the Christian.

(Naomi Reed Rhode)

> **Give God time to reveal Himself to you. Give yourself time to be silent and quiet before Him, waiting to receive, through the Spirit, the assurance of His presence with you, His power working in you.**
>
> *Andrew Murray*

If the Bible were to be destroyed and you could have only one page, which one would it be? A favorite text? The 23rd Psalm? Isaiah 53? The Nativity? The Sermon on the Mount? Some parables?

I believe I'd take the story of the walk to Emmaus. It is full of religious insight. It is authentic. It never fails. I want to paint a mental picture of it for you. When weary and dejected, we can turn to it and there a friend stands by our side. The words thrill us. A radiant personal Christ teaches us. His footsteps sound anew. It shows there is tenderness behind tragedy, and love beside the deepest shadows.

For millions, this passage has taken the loneliness out of the road toward the sunset. At the end, there is no bleak silence, but a sacrament: the bread of blessing broken by a hand broken for me.

It was at eventide when Jesus and the two men with whom he had been walking reached Emmaus. Jesus planned to go further, but they invited Him to stay with them. What would have happened if they hadn't invited Him? They would have missed seeing the risen, living Christ.

This same living Christ created Christianity, and no one or nothing else can keep it alive—not His teaching, not His works, but He Himself. This scene in Emmaus is not a page of ancient history, but a picture of abiding reality. Through all generations since that day, Christ has appeared unto men, just as He did then.

In times of struggle, need, tragedy, joy, He is there, talking with us along the road. But too often, we don't recognize Him until He is about to leave. Too few invite Him to abide. But Christ will abide with us only long enough to bless our bread. If we would abide with Him, we must be pilgrims too, following where there is no path, save that made by His feet.

Today, whether men admit it or not, there is a yearning for the presence of Christ, for the guest at the cottage door of Emmaus. Christ is here with us today, as he was with those disciples on the road 2,000 years ago. But the number of wistful worshippers at the altar of the unknown god is far too great. Some are in church, carried along by momentum and habit, but perplexed, while there at their side unrecognized stands the Jesus who blessed and broke the bread for the disciples at Emmaus.

Some take refuge in music, some in revolt, some in speculation, some in riches, some in pleasure, and some in even helping others. But they leave the surest help untried, the one who would walk with them along the road and open unto them the scriptures.

Has your heart recently been warmed by His company? Has He walked with you by the wayside? Christ is the "Yes" of God to all yearnings of humanity. In Him love finds fulfillment. How much we would have lost if this Emmaus story had never been recorded.

Into our lives one day, Jesus entered. Like Wesley's experience, our hearts were strangely warmed. But what has happened since? Does he dwell within us even now?

No one else can answer that question for you. But if it's still in the negative, remember that there stands by your very own door, not only at eventide but always, the same Christ who said, "Behold, I stand at the door and knock. If any man hears my voice, and will open the door, I will come in and sup with him."

(Excerpted from a message by Virgil Reed, date unknown.)

Naomi Responds

God's purpose for you is that you depend on Him and
His power NOW; that you see Him walking on the
waves—no shore in sight, no success, just the absolute
certainty that it is all right because you see Him.

Oswald Chambers

Early 20th century American artist Warner Sallman painted
many works that hold our hearts in wonder at the memory of
Christ's presence here on earth. He depicted Jesus standing at
the door knocking, walking on the Emmaus Road, and in his best-
known work, "Head of Christ."

Several of these paintings graced our home when I was a child.
Thus, the memory of those images has impressed upon my heart for
a lifetime the reality of His indwelling spirit in my life.

I can 'see' Jesus, walking with the two men on the road to
Emmaus—because He walks with me. I can feel the 'burning of their
hearts,' because mine burns too, and the thrill of having Him in my
home, and "opening the Scriptures" to me is a genuine ongoing life
experience.

I'm fascinated by the question my father asked in this message:
"If the Bible were to be destroyed and you could have only one page,
which one would it be?" I'd never thought of that concept before.

I'm even more awed by his own choice, his underscoring of the
personal relationship that is at the very heart of the Gospel, the good
news of the incarnate Christ. Christ's presence when we're weary,
dejected, needing comfort, needing perspective in our hurting
worlds, is not only promised, but is reality for the Christian.

I wonder if I consistently live as if He's dwelling within me,
warming my heart, and revealing the Scriptures to me daily. Is there
compassion for others? Is there grace, mercy, and tender wisdom in
my personal interactions? Is there the passion for others to know of
this 'presence' also?

And, beyond reveling in the personal comfort of our walk with
Jesus, is the awareness of the price He paid for this offer of abiding
always with us? The nail-scarred hands that hold our faltering, needy

hands belong to the One who came to die, for our sin. They assure us of his sacrifice, and His resurrection. They promise to hold us, and redeem us. They encompass our souls and are large enough for any aching heart to reside in their embrace.

And, the miracle of all miracles is the ever-abiding Holy Spirit, who never ever leaves us once we've opened the door to the inner sanctum of our very being.

For years, we chose to not have a doorknob on the front door of our home. Only those who knocked and for whom we opened the door from the inside could gain entrance. And, yes, we were often asked, "Why no doorknob?"

The reason was the extension of the reality of His waiting for us to open the door of our lives wide, wide to His love, grace and guidance, wide to share with others His love and compassion.

Chapter
20
Playing Second Fiddle

"One of the two which heard John speak and followed him, was Andrew, Simon Peter's brother."

John 1:40

Andrew took second place graciously, aware that a smaller place doesn't mean a smaller man. Greatness of position is no proof of greatness of soul.

(Virgil Reed)

If there were an "Andrew Award," to be given to someone in your family, your church, your neighborhood, your place of business, who would it be?

(Naomi Reed Rhode)

It is amazing what you can accomplish if you do not care who gets the credit.

Harry S. Truman

Who is that man, arm-in-arm with a friend who is following Jesus? One might reply, "Why, that's Andrew. I thought everybody knew him. He led Simon Peter to Jesus. He was the first disciple won by Jesus. He leads millions—a great man—that's Andrew."

But that was not the answer. Instead the answer was, "Let me think. Oh, he is Andrew, just Simon Peter's brother." Andrew hardly had a reputation of his own. What little he had was in his brother's name.

Perhaps he often thought of sending in his resignation and of going back to his fishing. Perhaps he felt he'd rather be first in a little boat on the Sea of Galilee than playing second fiddle among the Apostles. But Andrew got used to "second fiddle" and always played it well.

Andrew, like most of us, failed to make the first team. All of us must play second fiddle sometime, somewhere. Andrew didn't choose to play "second fiddle." He had a right to expect first place, for he was first to become a disciple.

Andrew was a member of a quartet—Peter, James, John and Andrew. Peter, James, John—in first place. Andrew was always left out. These four played together as boys, went to the same synagogue, and were partners in a fishing business, facing dangers and storms together. Now they were engaged in their highest adventure and Andrew was forced to play second fiddle.

When Jesus went to the home of Jairus to bring his daughter back to life, He allowed no one to go in with Him except the child's parents, and Peter, James and John. As usual, Andrew was left out.

What did he do? He didn't grow bitter. Andrew took second place graciously, aware that a smaller place doesn't mean a smaller man. Greatness of position is no proof of greatness of soul. Jesus Himself declared that, "the first shall be last and the last first."

Are all trees giant redwoods? Are all birds ostriches? Are all flowers century plants? God loves variety, and has a place for all. A hummingbird in His sight is as great as an ostrich.

Andrew lived victoriously. Having found Jesus, he shared that good news with others, becoming an evangelist in his own household, as he immediately went to his own brother, Simon, explained what he had experienced, and brought him to Jesus. Later, when Jesus sought a way to feed the multitude who had followed Him, it was Andrew who found the boy with the loaves and fishes.

Andrew was willing to play the part assigned to him. God is the bandmaster, and we must learn to play well our assigned instrument.

In this matter of living for Christ, play well. The first fiddle, second fiddle, or any other instrument, has its place. Played to the best of one's ability and according to the printed notes, it makes for music that pleases the ear of the Great Director of the music of the earth.

Perhaps you are a Peter, James or John. Perhaps you're *only* an Andrew. But remember that it was Andrew who found the Christ, and then showed others the way.

(Excerpted from a message by Virgil Reed, date unknown.)

Naomi Responds

The smaller we are, the more room God has for us.

Croft M. Pentz

How I love this excerpt from my Dad's message! It makes me smile, and it makes me applaud—applaud those who play 'second fiddle'—the Andrews in life! They're everywhere—substitute teachers, back-up musicians, second-string team members, runners-up, silver medalists—doing their jobs with little fanfare or applause.

Then we examine the life of Andrew again, perhaps more closely. Remember that it was Andrew who found the Christ, and then, as we read in the Gospel of John, "The first thing Andrew did was to find his brother Simon and tell him: 'We have found the Messiah'" (John 1:41).

What powerful words! What an incredible concept: to point the way to Jesus, to the Master, to the Healer, to the Christ, to the Son of God! Is there a higher calling?

There are so many contemporary 'Andrews,' men and women who faithfully and quietly take care of their responsibilities, day in and day out, in every field of human endeavor. But the Andrews I want to highlight, herald and extol are the stay-at-home mothers—the faithful women who set aside their formal education, their professional ambitions and careers, their climbing the ladder of earthly acclaim, to raise their children. Diapers, dishes and discipline are part of a daily parade of unending duties—duties which parallel the honor of encouraging dreams, sharing days, and teaching values.

I honor my mother for forfeiting the scholastic rewards of teaching for bandaging knees, baking, cleaning, caring, and teaching child evangelism classes in our home. It was at one of these classes that, as the age of six, I asked Jesus to be my Lord and Savior.

I honor my daughters, Katherine, with a degree in Psychology from Westmont College, and Beth with a Doctorate in Dentistry from Loma Linda, for staying home raising children who study music, learn chess, languages, and read/read/read, discovering God's best for their lives at the knee of Andrews who are content with playing 'second fiddle.'

And I honor many of my dear sisters in Christ, and close friends, who have done the same through the years. Much like Andrew, these dear people are seemingly playing 'second fiddle', and yet—they're the ones who are responsible for finding the Christ, and showing others the way! They are responsible for building a legacy of faith for the next generation of Americans who will in turn gladly play 'second fiddle' to their own children.

And then I think of the call on your life and mine. Andrew was an "evangelist" in his own household, immediately seeking out his brother Simon to tell him about finding the Messiah. There's nothing more thrilling for Jim and for me than knowing that our three children know and love the Lord. Nothing gives us more joy than knowing that their spouses love the Lord, and that our 12 grandchildren are following Jesus!

Indeed Andrew lived victoriously! And I'm thrilled to follow his lead, his passion to share the good news with others, and to lead them to the Christ!

Have you met some "Andrews," quiet heroes who were there, behind the scenes, having an impact in your life, perhaps pointing you in a direction you might otherwise have missed? If there were an "Andrew Award," to be given to someone in your family, your church, your neighborhood, your place of business, who would it be? You may have one or many people to nominate, and then be sure to thank God for the positive impact each one has had on your life's journey.

Chapter
21

Is Your Religion Dry? – Or Does Your Face Shine?

"One thing I do know. I was blind but now I see!"

John 9:25

A good way to change dry religion into a blessed one is to meet up with the Savior and have him lighten your load and touch your eyes.

(Virgil Reed)

Is my "religion" as worn as a dusty, antiquated coat of useless rags? Or does the light of His grace, love and mercy flow through my face, my countenance into a dark and hurting world?

(Naomi Reed Rhode)

> **A true Christian's enthusiasm for the Lord Jesus Christ should be so exuberant that it would be far more likely to set others on fire than to be extinguished by worldly influences.**
>
> *Henrietta C. Mears*

No merely formal, routine religion can help us much in these times. Many of us acknowledge that our own personal experience of religion and Christianity has often been conventional—inherited beliefs—opinions into which we argued ourselves—observances of worship on which we were brought up. Much so-called religion is thus second hand and as dry as dust.

Over against such religion, we set the story of today's lesson, the story of the blind man Jesus healed. He told the Pharisees, "One thing I do know. I was blind but now I see!" This is the genuine article in spiritual experience, a man seeing something so clearly that nothing can make him deny it.

In this Gospel, the Apostle John presented Jesus vividly. The story of the raising of Lazarus is all about the life-giver. The story of the giving of sight to this blind man is all about the light-bringer. The blind man said, Jesus may be this or that, and your opinions may be thus or so, but one thing I personally know, "I was blind but now I see!"

How superficial belief can be, but to see life as Jesus saw it, to look at people and money and friendship and trouble and death, as he looked at them, that would not be superficial. Then we could say with the blind man in our story, "One thing I do know. I was blind but now I see!"

Zacchaeus, the tax gatherer, the woman of Samaria, Mary Magdalene, and all the rest, had seen life one way before Jesus crossed their paths. But after meeting with the Master, they could never see life the same again. Jesus transformed their lives, and filled them with power. Jesus had that same effect upon his first disciples; he opened their eyes to a new way of looking at life.

In this regard, Jesus was an artist. For this is what an artist does. He doesn't argue. He paints a picture and says, "See!" Jesus seldom argued. He told the story of the Prodigal Son, and then he said, "See!" He told the story of the five wise and five foolish virgins, and showed the tragedy of being unprepared, and then he simply said one word, "See!" He told the story of the Good Samaritan who helped a stranger in need, and he asked, "Can you not see?"

That's genuine Christianity—nothing formal and dry as dust about that. Is your religion dry? I know that in our youth, formal creeds seemed as dry as dust and ashes, but when we meet up with the Master, the scene changes.

The faith of this blind man had made him whole. He was convinced beyond a shadow of a doubt. He didn't claim to know everything. He simply knew he was healed, and testified to the fact and to the Christ. From that time forward, there must have shone from the face of that blind man a radiance that couldn't be mistaken.

A good way to change dry religion into a blessed one is to meet up with the Savior and have him lighten your load and touch your eyes. How fine it would be to have fewer people with dry-as-powder religion, and with faces through which the light of God's love could shine into this world.

"One thing I do know. I was blind but now I see."

(Excerpted from a message by Virgil Reed, date unknown.)

Naomi Responds

The way at times seems dark, but light will arise, if thou trust in the Lord, and wait patiently for Him.

Elizabeth T. King

It's so easy to focus on my needs, my goals, my purpose in life, instead of truly "seeing" Christ's life, death, resurrection and indwelling Spirit which provides the purpose, "the seeing," which always precede the doing and being of my life.

Jesus was like a magnet. People were drawn to Him out of curiosity, difficulty, damaged lives, and distressing situations. Many of them were transformed, becoming change agents in their worlds, 'shining faces' illuminated by new vision.

We recently shared in the homegoing of my husband Jim's mother, Agnes Rhode Mesenburg. Her repeated theme to us in her 95th year was her desire to go and be in the presence of Jesus. There was no fear, no "dry religion," only the clear vision of eternity in mansions prepared for her. It was truly as if she could see heaven.

A few days before she died, she asked me to go ahead and open the gates for her. Startled, I asked if she really meant for me to die ahead of her. "Oh, no, I just want you to stand and hold the gates open for me, get a glimpse of what glory I will experience." You can do that through prayer, was her firm confirmation of faith and hope.

I believe she wanted me to "see" the glory, to anticipate the presence of Jesus she would experience and know firsthand very soon.

Our sweet granddaughter, Kylin, was comforted in the process of losing her great grandmother by 'seeing' her leaving, as a ship leaves the shore—getting further and further away from this life, and closer and closer to the horizon of a new world. As we were saying goodbye with the sadness of losing her, those on the other side were welcoming her to her eternal home.

The triumph, the beauty, the amazing reality of our faith is that once we were blind, now we see. And 'then,' we will see more clearly, more gloriously, more triumphantly, with the brilliant light of His eternal love, the home prepared for us, surrounded by the shining faces of His people and perfected grace.

That will be 'then'—this is here, and now! Is my "religion" as worn as a dusty, antiquated coat of useless rags? Or does the light of His grace, love and mercy flow through my face, my countenance into a dark and hurting world?

It's not about me—or about you. It is all about Him! "I was blind but now I see." Have your eyes been opened by the Savior? Do you see Him? If not, allow Him to take away your blindness, and let His light shine from your newly opened eyes.

Chapter
22

Mistaken Tears

"Daughters of Jerusalem, weep not for me, but weep for yourselves, and for your children."

Luke 23:28

These were mistaken tears for the Christ on the cross, instead of tears for those who reject the salvation He freely offers.

(Virgil Reed)

How easy it is for us to sympathetically care about the pain we observe in the world. But how difficult it is to rather see deep into souls, to the underlying challenges they face and a lasting solution, instead of a temporary cure.

(Naomi Reed Rhode)

Tears shed for self are tears of weakness, but tears shed for others are a sign of strength.

Billy Graham

If ever there was a just cause for tears, it would seem to be here—Jesus on the way to Calvary. The streets are jammed with curious people who, for the most part, are hostile to Jesus. They ridicule and insult the man who threatens at any moment to fall under the weight of a too heavy cross.

While the faces of most of the crowd are unfriendly, there are some exceptions. There are a few women who are sorry to see Him being led to a ghastly death. They say, "He's so young, so innocent. He was so kind. He has done no wrong." They are sorry for him, and they burst into tears.

The reaction of Jesus is surprising. He doesn't seem to appreciate these tears. Yet no man was more appreciative than Jesus. Did He not say that even a glass of cold water given in his name would not go unrewarded?

A few days earlier, Jesus had been shown kindness by a woman while he was at a dinner party, anointing His head with expensive perfume. When the disciples objected, Jesus said, "Wherever this story shall be told through out the whole world it shall be in memory of her kind deed." Of course Jesus appreciated kindness and consideration, but why did He not appreciate these misplaced tears?

The real reason is that Jesus sees that these women have missed the real point of the tragedy. Theirs are mistaken tears. They are right about shedding tears, but they are weeping for a wrong cause. They are sobbing over Jesus, when they ought to be sobbing over themselves and their children.

Jesus does not consider Himself an object of pity. He rather declares that the women themselves and their children are the ones who are to be pitied. No wonder then that Jesus says, "Weep not for me, but weep for yourselves and your children."

Mistaken tears. Mistaken ideas. We have them aplenty. The hell, about which our fathers spoke so fervently, seems to have cooled off so much that it would make a fairly good summer resort.

Do you think a loving God would send even the worst man to hell? "No!" I would answer, but I am sure there are many men living in a hell of their own making. God will never send any man to hell, but many men send themselves there.

Do you think, someone asks, that God will punish a man for a false belief? Certainly not, and yet I know of a man who was convinced he could live without eating and drinking. He was sincere, so sincere that he bet his life on his false faith. But, in spite of the goodness of God and the sincerity of his faith, he became a walking skeleton, fainted and went into a coma. All that saved him from death was forced feeding.

When a man refuses to obey the laws of physical health he must suffer. If we neglect to take bread we die. Even so, we die spiritually when we fail to avail ourselves of the Bread of Life. And *there is no forced feeding*. This is not a theory; it is a plain everyday fact.

Jesus needed no tears shed for Him. Was He not doing the will of God? He was not losing his life; he was giving it. He forbids the tears of these sincere women, because he is living victoriously.

These were mistaken tears for the Christ on the cross, instead of tears for those who reject the salvation He freely offers. For there is in this life but one superlative tragedy: that is to miss knowing God through Jesus.

He is our only hope for the life that now is, and for the life to come. May God help us to believe it, and to accept it.

(Excerpted from a message by Virgil Reed, date unknown.)

Naomi Responds

You are Christ to the world. Christ has no hands but your hands to touch and bless and heal, no feet but your feet to lead men in the path of truth, no arms but your arms to gather the scattered, no tongue but your tongues to cheer a suffering mankind, no heart but your heart to love, to pity, to care.

Saint Francis of Assisi

As I reflected on this passage of Scripture, I couldn't help thinking that it seemed so unlike Jesus to rebuke the tears of those compassionate women along the Via Dolorosa. After all, the Bible describes Him as "a man of sorrows and acquainted with grief." And when He came to the tomb of his friend Lazarus, His reaction is described in the shortest verse in all of Scripture: "Jesus wept" (John 11:35). Clearly He had come to identify with our sorrows and our tears.

Certainly these women, and many others in that mob lining the streets, must have felt the same way. Here was Jesus, this innocent man, still bearing the wounds from the terrible beatings, with bloody thorn-punctured brow, carrying his own cross, struggling and stumbling past them. Was He not thought by many of them to be the promised Messiah? Certainly, He was well deserving of their sorrow and tears.

And then came the astonishing reply: "Daughters of Jerusalem, weep not for me, but weep for yourselves, and for your children." He needed no tears shed for Him! He was doing the will of His Father. They were not taking His life, He was giving it! He was not a victim, but the victor!

One wonders with amazement that He would even notice the women weeping. Amidst the jeers, and in spite of His terrible suffering, he saw their tears. But even more, He saw into their very hearts. Even in His last hours on earth, He was "about His Father's business," pointing people to their own need for forgiveness and grace, and away from their sympathy for His physical suffering.

His directness could shock us, or serve as a powerful reminder of our role in the lives of others. His statement to the women went far beyond a reprimand, to a deep personal, spiritual concern for them and for their children—and for a hurting world.

How easy it is for us to sympathetically care about the pain we observe in the world. But how difficult it is to rather see deep into souls, to the underlying challenges they face and a lasting solution, instead of a temporary cure.

Does Jesus care about our tears? Oh, yes! Scripture twice refers to Him wiping away our tears. He cares! But He wants our tears to be directed to those who are lost, who are hurting, who are without eternal hope, who are without a Shepherd, a Savior, who reject the purpose of the cross: to take away "the sins of the world."

Are my tears 'mistaken,' or do they count in His eternal plan?

Chapter
23

The Abiding City

"For we have not here an abiding city, but we seek after the city which is to come."

Hebrews 13:14

Though the earth be changed, and though the mountains be cast into the sea, there is still one abiding city.

(Virgil Reed)

I'm looking forward to one day occupying the home Jesus has already prepared for me in that 'abiding city.'

(Naomi Reed Rhode)

Life's a voyage that's homeward bound.

Herman Melville

History may be thought to be a stage on which a drama is played, and the "actors" spend their lives trying to keep abreast of the changes that keep coming. No sooner has the child become accustomed to childhood than he finds he has changed—he has become an adult.

Family responsibilities crop up, and when he has struggled under this new change until he is finally in a position to enjoy his children, they are grown up and ready to leave home.

It often feels that by the time we become well regulated, change comes along to disrupt things. How often men have been forced to bow under the crushing load of change.

We would like security. There is a desire in all of us to anchor our possessions. We buy insurance to prepare for any changes that might come. If fire strikes our homes, the change doesn't wipe us out. People who retire make provisions for continued income, so the change caused by old age won't affect their ability to survive during the years when they can't work.

But even here, many are thwarted because of the rise in the cost of living, and the lesson is driven home that we have not here an abiding city. Many buy life insurance, so that when the final change comes, those left behind are not too seriously affected financially.

In all of life, death comes to interrupt. New people are on their way to take our place on this earth. Oh, we have not here an abiding city, but we look for that city which is to come, and there we shall stand in the presence of God, who changes not.

Because we have not here an abiding city, our final hope is not resting upon this earth. It shall be anchored in that city which is to come. Though the earth be changed, and though the mountains be cast into the sea, there is still one abiding city. Toward that city we would cast our vision today.

All change is not a curse. If things were to grind to a stop as they are this moment, or as they were just a week ago, life would be unbearable for many. Some would go on with endless suffering, with no chance for recovery, as there could be no change for the better.

Jesus Christ walked the face of this earth. It was His mission to experience the same changes we do, finally even the change called death. But having gone through that change, He entered into a life that does not change, because the God who changes not has decreed that it shall never change.

So with our eyes on the Christ who has taken the sting and the sorrow from the grave, and has decreed that we too shall one day rise with Him, we look to that city which is to come.

Pessimists have sometimes called this life "a vale of tears." And there is truth there, for there is much sorrow on this old earth. One pessimist called this earth "the city of dreadful night." Such an attitude is true only for those who build all their hope and confidence on this world, learning to dread that we have not here an abiding city, and failing to look to that city which is to come. For them there is nothing left to do but to call such an earth a "city of dreadful night," for such it is.

Instead, we stand here today, not without hope, but anchored in the love and mercy of God, knowing that here we have not an abiding city, but we look for that city which to come.

(Excerpted from a message by Virgil Reed, date unknown.)

Naomi Responds

Without the destination in view, we easily lose our way...So what is our destination? Our destination is home with our Father in heaven. It is so easy on this journey to lose sight of our destination and to focus on the detours of this life instead. This life is only the trip to get home.

Dr. Bob Snyder

This world is not my home, I'm just a'passin' through. If heaven's not my home, then Lord what will I do?" We sing the refrain with gladness. We picture streets of gold, and mansions untold. And yet, the reality of this earthly home, this human body, these sometimes difficult relationships, sorrows and pain are real, really real!

Having been in the professional world of speaking for more than 30 years, I have the interesting experience of meeting people who heard me speak decades ago. Their gracious greetings after hearing me speak "again, after all these years" usually includes some variation of this statement: "You haven't changed at all. Oh my, this life has been good to you, etc., etc."

Certainly these statements are complimentary. And I certainly cherish the hope that there may be a thread of truth in them, mixed with the reality of their own distorted perspective and poor eyesight.

And, yet, I trust that I have changed! I trust that my experience of God's abundance over the intervening years—the goodness of family, the grace of purpose in my life, the blessing of health, the wonder of travel, the gift of friendship, and the passion for those who do not know His love—are signs of indelible change. I trust that the home He has entrusted me with here has been a blessing to the next generation: 12 sweet grandchildren, and an abundance of travelers across my stage of life.

And mostly, I trust that the eternal home being readied for me is furnished with joy unspeakable because of His presence, and the treasure of souls whose lives have passed my way.

I've lived long enough to see buildings that have been built, used, and torn down. I've lived long enough to see marriages that seemed strong and healthy be dissolved in sadness and pain. I've seen healthy bodies become weak with the rampages of disease and death. I've lived to be glad often that this world is 'not my home'!

And yet, I've been privileged to see people's lives changed from hopelessness to radiant joy, from purposeless boredom to eternal perspective, from chaos to peace, from hatred to love, from addictive behavior to victorious sobriety.

These are all celebrating in the most positive sense this 'passing world,' and preparing for the eternal and abiding city that awaits.

I remember with some humor a rather eccentric elderly lady asking my friend for the 'new address' of her mother, who had just passed away. She wanted to change the street address in her address book to the plot number in the cemetery. My friend's radiant, knowing response was to point her heavenward!

Truly, her mother's body was 'resting' in a grave, but her spirit, ah, her spirit, her very being, was and is for eternity in the promised 'abiding city,' forever reigning with her Lord.

I'm looking forward to one day occupying the home Jesus has already prepared for me in that 'abiding city.' Want to be neighbors?

Chapter
24
God's Endless Quest

"The eyes of the Lord run to and fro throughout the whole earth, to show himself strong in behalf of those whose heart is perfect toward him."

2 Chronicles 16:9

God is willing to pay any price for man, even to the price of his only begotten son. God's heartache for man is told in the story of the cross.

(Virgil Reed)

These echoes of God's love are evident throughout Scripture. As far as we may wander, He is there. He is calling, He is caring, and He will welcome us home.

(Naomi Reed Rhode)

I didn't find God—He found me. Religions teach man's search for God, and the gospel teaches God's search for man.

E. Stanley Jones

The book of Second Chronicles is very prosaic, but here it bursts into beautiful and exquisite poetry. The Gospel shown here is as fresh and bracing as that of the New Testament. The text heartens us because of the light it flashes upon the face of the Lord. It shows him as the eternal seeker after man.

It throws light upon God's face, and also upon the face of Man. It tells us something we are so prone to forget: that man, in spite of his follies, faults and sins, is still a grand creature. Man is akin to the beasts, I know, but he also has that which makes him closely akin to God.

Pessimists would have us agree with the cynic who said, "I could believe in humanity if it were not for the folks." There is no trust man has not betrayed. There is no crime man has not committed. There is no depth of moral infamy he has not reached. At man's worst, he seems the very son of Satan.

And yet, if pessimism says there is nothing too bad to say about man, optimism says there is nothing too good to say about man. There is no danger he has not dared. There is no sacrifice he has not been glad to make. He has crossed all seas and penetrated all forests. Man: so much clay; so much fine gold. Man: son of Adam, son of God.

One mark of man's greatness is his insatiable hunger for God. All other creatures are content with the satisfaction of physical needs. The Prodigal Son spent all he had, and ate with the swine. The swine were satisfied and could lie down and sleep, but the Prodigal was ill at ease and longed for home.

The Psalmist wrote: "As the hart panteth after the water brooks, so panteth my soul after Thee, O God." Just as eagles are made to soar in the upper air above the storms, so are we made for God and cannot rest without Him.

Yet, the supreme mark of our greatness is not our hunger for God but God's hunger for us. We seek because we are sought; we love because He first loved us. Man is therefore a great creature, so precious that even at his worst he outweighs the world.

On the first page of the Bible, we find God searching for man, calling out, "Adam, where art thou?" And on the last page, we read, "And the Spirit and the Bride say 'Come'."

God's quest for man reached its climax in the ministry of his Son Jesus, "who is come to seek and save that which is lost." God is willing to pay any price for man, even to the price of his only begotten son. God's heartache for man is told in the story of the cross.

What shall you and I do about this seeking God? Shall we let Him find us even more so today than ever before? It is your King who knocks at your door. It is your King who is seeking you.

(Excerpted from a message by Virgil Reed, date unknown.)

Naomi Responds

**Sin had no sooner come into the world than God came
in Grace seeking the sinner, and so from the first
question, "Adam, where art thou?" on to the
incarnation, God has been speaking to man.**

Harry A. Ironside

I'm hiding; come and find me!" All parents have an echo of that refrain in their souls forever. The 'game' started when our children were babies. Innocently they covered their eyes, as if blocking out their existence, and wondered if we could see or even imagine where they were. As they became toddlers, we remember their gleeful refrain, over and over, as they'd run, hiding in obvious proximity and then inviting us to find them.

As teenagers, driver's license 'in hand,' the quest was driving somewhere unexpected—beyond the perimeter of our knowledge—and wondering if we'd ever know, or care.

As adults—oh, how many heartaches have been created by the increasing departures from the safety, the love, and the parental arms of those who never stop caring, into relationships, endeavors, and addictions that harm and destroy homes, families and society.

As I reflected on this message of my father's, I was again awed by my Heavenly Father's message to me. From the first page of Scripture to the last, His quest is 'the central theme' of Holy Word—"Come unto me..." "I will never leave you or forsake you..." "The eyes of the Lord search to and fro throughout the earth..." "Prepare a feast.....my son who was lost, has been found!"

These echoes of God's love are evident throughout Scripture. As far as we may wander, He is there. He is calling, He is caring, and He will welcome us home.

These are the echoes of His love which then blaze the mandate for our parental love. We see this story played out in the tragedies of lives around us daily—children leaving, hurting, lost—and parents seeking, caring and loving far beyond reasonability.

I recently reread Henri Nouwen's amazing book, *The Return of the Prodigal Son*. As he ponders the deep significance of Rembrandt's rendition of this biblical parable, he identifies with each of the figures portrayed in this amazing painting: the shame, humility, and penitence of the returning son; the judgment, arrogance, and superiority of the older brother; the compassion, forgiveness and love of the father.

Nouwen's closing challenge for us is to be like 'the father' in our attitude toward those who have wandered, hurt, and denied our love.

The irony of such a challenge is so evident. We seek only because we are sought.

We love only because He first loved us.

His pattern of loving, seeking, finding is modeled, molded, and melded into our very fiber as His children. And only with His love can we love to this unfathomable extent.

How often have you heard the voice on the phone, "Mom, Dad, are you there? I need you!"

Reminiscent? Oh, yes—of the many times we call: "Father, Father, are you there? I need you!"

And He is always there!

Chapter
25
The Little Foxes

"Catch for us the foxes, the little foxes which spoil
the vines."

Song of Solomon 2:15

My friends, as fellow Christians and members of the church of Christ, beware the foxes, the little foxes that spoil the vine.

(Virgil Reed)

It's the power of the little things, the seemingly insignificant acts, words, insinuations that can tear down, and destroy products, health, relationships, and institutions.

(Naomi Reed Rhode)

No sin is small. It is against an infinite God, and may have consequences immeasurable. No grain of sand is small in the mechanism of a watch.

Jeremy Taylor

(Note: As a Boy Scout executive, Virgil Reed was transferred from Fargo, North Dakota to South St. Paul, Minnesota in September 1948. The following is excerpted from his farewell message to his congregation on leaving the Fargo area.)

Centuries ago in Palestine, the chief occupation was tending the grape vines and the manufacture and sale of the juice from the ripened fruit. But something happened to upset the process and mar the tranquility of the people. It was a plague, not of locusts or frogs, but of something quite as destructive.

Things that destroy are not always terrible to look upon and, in this case, the plague which came to destroy the source of income for these early people was not of ugly things, but cunning, cute, playful "little foxes." The big foxes, who stole the grapes, were easily seen and chased away, but the little foxes did more damage. Harder to see, they nibbled away at the tender roots of the grape vine and killed the entire vine.

We are leaving this community and our parting wish for you is that God will save you from "the little foxes which spoil the vines." We tend to focus on the big things and often forget the little foxes, the ones which can cause the most damage.

There was a giant tree in Estes Park, Colorado that was 500 years old. It had been struck by lightning 11 times and survived. It had experienced three major landslides and lived on. Then a tiny little beetle bored its way into that giant of a tree and killed it.

My friends, as fellow Christians and members of the church of Christ, beware the foxes, the little foxes that spoil the vine. Beware the loose tongue, the thoughtless statement, the little things that cunningly slip by, and are in outward appearance as playful as a little fox puppy. They are the ones that spoil the vines and ruin our chances of a blessed eternity.

"Dear Lord, we praise Thee for this occasion, for friends, for Thy love, Thy Word and Thy promises. May we, as we part, remember that though we are apart by miles we are one with Thee. Bless us as we go our several ways. Save us from the little foxes that spoil the vines. Amen!"

Naomi Responds

**The tongue is but three inches long, yet it can kill
a man six feet high.**

Japanese Proverb

Just a few extra calories; just a bit too much salt; just a slightly wrong turn; just a tiny lie—or one more drink! It's the little things, the "Little Foxes" in life, that make all the difference.

One of my Dad's favorite stories was of the French Creole concept of *lagniappe*—giving every bit you were paid for, and then 'just a little bit more,' which makes all the difference in life, in a positive way.

Isn't it interesting that the same is true in the negative sense! It's the power of the little things, the seemingly insignificant acts, words, insinuations that can tear down, and destroy products, health, relationships, and institutions.

Scripture speaks of the tongue as being one of the most destructive parts of our bodies. Certainly our words are as crafty, hurtful, and harmful as the wildest hurricane or fire.

Years ago, a friend said to me, "Naomi, words become frozen reality." Being a lover of words, their meaning, delivery, eloquence, power, might, and beauty, that phrase has always intrigued me.

Each of us has etched in our souls "little foxes," words that have become frozen reality, and tend to sabotage our noblest thoughts and efforts at times of greatest testing.

My father gave this short exhortation as he left his volunteer church ministry to further his professional career as a Boy Scout executive in another area of the country. I've thought about why he'd choose this message as the summation of his ministry, and challenge for the future of his congregation (and his own).

I believe it's because he too was a lover of words, a master at communication skills, and realized the power of the tongue to mold attitudes, actions, and outcomes. Words can be used to manipulate or to minister, to build up or to tear down.

He had experienced the 'little things' that creep in and destroy. He cherished the Body of Christ. He wanted that part of the vineyard he'd been privileged to be caretaker for to be healthy.

His words have lived on! Today, more than half a century later, I'm blessed to hear his words echo in my life, and in the lives of our three children and 12 grandchildren. And they've echoed through 30 years of my speaking on platforms throughout this country and around the world. Just a tiny pebble—but the ripples are eternal.

My father's closing prayer for his people was: "We are apart by miles, but one with Thee."

How apropos, Dad! You have given so much to me, to pass on to others. We're apart briefly by death, but joined forever by His life. Thank you, Dad. How I look forward to spending eternity with you—and with the Lord you loved and served so faithfully.

So, dear reader and friend, thank you for allowing us to share these messages from the pen and heart of my father, Virgil Asbury Reed, and my responses. I pray you've gleaned some wisdom and inspiration from his thoughts, and formulated a response of your own that will lead to action.

The book of Revelation speaks of the "grandstand of the saints....cheering us on." I have no doubt that Virgil Reed is in that grandstand. And I have no doubt that he is cheering us on, in this journey of choice to honor our highest and best calling.

Most importantly, I know that God the Father is patiently loving us throughout our journey, and leading us home.

Epilogue

The phone rang and I heard her expectant voice say, "Mom, I think it's time!" Time! That illusive commodity that goes too slow, too fast, and sometimes literally seems to 'stand still.'

We'd had all tried to be patient these last few days, as we awaited this fourth child, in what was to be a family of six children. The months had gone quickly since we heard the wonderful news that another baby was to be born. But now, the days were hanging in anticipation for this birth.

My rush to be of encouragement was not a rush down the freeway to the hospital, but a quick one-mile drive to the home of our daughter and son-in-law, Beth and Curt Hamann.

This was to be a different kind of birthing experience. Curt, a physician, and Beth had decided on a home delivery, and had asked me to be the only other person to assist our precious daughter in this birth.

What a privilege! Was I ready for this experience? The experience of a new life being birthed in the quiet, tender beauty of a home, a bedroom with soft music, quiet encouragement and the peaceful, purposeful worthy work of labor and delivery?

The miracle of new life/birth! Never was it more amazing to me—*sans* the sterile, rush, hustle and mystery of hospital routine—filled with confidence, peace and pure joy of new life.

After three boys, the cry of this new life, this precious baby girl, Kylin Katherine, was almost indescribable joy. As tears of gratitude were shed, those sweet little boys were invited in to share in the awe. A brand new person had been born into our lives. That sweet warm body was lying on a tired Mommy's tummy. The oldest brother, Dathan, was invited to 'cut the cord,' as Dad's gloved hands guided his young bold hand.

I stood, camera in hand, and took 'the picture'—a picture of hands. A mother's tender hand being clutched by the finger of a new precious baby girl. A father's gloved hand and a brother's hand. Most important was the knowledge that the legacy of love, peace and joy were being passed to another generation by the Omnipotent Hands of our Heavenly Father.

"A Father's Hands," and "*The* Father's Hands,"—a legacy passed from generation to generation, a symbol of His grace, and plan for our lives. I wrote a poem about those cumulative 'hands,' placed the picture in an artist's rendition of "The Father's Hands," and framed it for posterity.

Given by Hands of Love

"You're on your own, you're on your own,
little girl" – the father said,

As competent, experienced, strong hands tied
the string around the umbilical cord.

"You're safely here and so very loved, little
girl" – the mother said,

As gentle, loving, sacrificial hands cradled her
new warm baby girl.

"You're so tiny, and now so really real, little
girl" – the little brother said,

As wondering, hesitant, learning hands cut the
strange looking cord.

"You're new, brand new, little girl" – your tiny
seeking, holding hand says,

As it reaches for family, warmth and comfort.

"You're created in my image, and known
before the foundation of the world, little girl" –
The Father said,

As omnipotent, omniscient, omnipresent hands
gave His child to this family, this world.

"Always come back, always come back, little
girl" – the Family of God says,

As praying, guiding, caring hands lead you to a
chosen position in His and our eternal family.

You are loved,
Kylin Katherine Hamann!
August 28, 1992
Love, Amma
…there at birth,
…there always!!

This symbol of God's love, "A Father's Hand," was exactly representative of God's faithfulness from generation to generation. The faithfulness that allowed me to be raised in a home that loved God the Father. A faithfulness that provided a father for my children with the same Godly wisdom and strength. And then, seeing our children raising their children in the same pattern!

My father died when I was 13 years old. Yet, his influence has impacted me every day of my life, spiritually, emotionally and intellectually. It has most certainly provided the pattern and passion for my life, primarily based on the framework of God's love and promises.

What better way to pass on His love than to pass on the love expressed in a father's touch, a mother's touch, a legacy of love from generation to generation. I invite you to join me on this journey of a father's influence.

> *We will tell the next generation the*
> *praiseworthy deeds of the LORD,*
> *his power, and the wonders he has*
> *done...so the next generation*
> *would know them, even the chil-*
> *dren yet to be born, and they in*
> *turn would tell their children. Then*
> *they would put their trust in God*
> *and would not forget his deeds but*
> *would keep his commands.*
>
> Psalm 78:4, 6-7

It is my prayer that your awareness, and passion for continuing influence on your children, grandchildren, nieces, nephews, friends and extended family will continue, and powerfully impact a hurting world.